The
Reference
Shelf

Rights to Privacy

Edited by Robert Emmet Long

The Reference Shelf
Volume 69 • Number 3

The H. W. Wilson Company
New York • Dublin
1997

The Reference Shelf

The books in this series contain reprints of articles, excerpts from books, and address-es on current issues and social trends in the United States and other countries. There are six separately bound numbers in each volume, all of which are generally published in the same calendar year. Numbers one through five are each devoted to a single sub-ject, providing background information and discussion from various points of view and concluding with a comprehensive bibliography that lists books, pamphlets and abstracts of additional articles on the subject. The final number of each volume is a collection of recent speeches. This number also contains a subject index to all the arti-cles in an entire Reference Shelf volume. Books in the series may be purchased indi-vidually or on subscription.

Visit H.W. Wilson's web site: http://www.hwwilson.com

Library of Congress Cataloging-in-Publication Data

Right to Privacy / edited by Robert Emmet Long.
    p.   cm. — (The reference shelf ; v. 69, no. 3)
    Includes bibliographical references and index.
    ISBN 0-8242-0916-8
    1. Privacy, Right of—United States. I. Long, Robert Emmet.
II. Series.
KF1262.R54 1997
342.73'0858—dc21
                                                  97-13914
                                                        CIP

Cover: A man is searched after walking through a metal detector.

Photo: AP/Wide World Photos

Printed in the United States of America

Contents

IV. Cyberspace Controversies

Bibliography

Preface

If this is the information age, then it is also the age of information gathering. People are inundated with all manner of information from the print and the broadcast media, and they themselves are the object of information procured on an unprecedented scale. This extensive procuring and disseminating of information about individuals' lives, of which they are often unaware, raises the question of the violation of privacy rights safeguarded in the Constitution. The dissemination of this data, moreover, may result in considerable injury to the party involved. His or her medical history, for example, may be sold to an insurance company, which might deny him or her coverage or impose greatly increased rates; and there is always the possibility that the medical report may be factually incorrect. The most personal facts of his or her professional or sexual life might be obtained by an employer and could very well be prejudicial. What is particularly surprising in the literature of privacy rights is the extent to which personal data about American citizens can be obtained and made available to interested parties. The issue, therefore, affects everyone, and has far-reaching implications concerning covert surveillance and the erosion of individual privacy in this country.

Section One of this compilation provides articles revealing the types of information about people that, whether they are aware of it or not, can be procured by credit bureaus and "superbureaus" and then sold by them to insurance companies and other businesses. Unlisted phone numbers can be obtained, for example, as well as bank records, work histories, criminal convictions, health reports, and Social Security earnings. This is made possible by the big computer databases that were unavailable even a generation ago. The first article in this section discloses the new potential that the public has against invasions of their privacy. Another article weighs the question of which should have priority—privacy interests or the welfare of the state. The final article discusses the importance of privacy, loss of privacy, and legal protection against that loss.

An aspect of the privacy issue having particular interest for the American Civil Liberties Union is privacy and the workplace, the subject of Section Two. In response to soaring insurance costs and other pressures involving worker productivity and industrial espionage, corporate America has stepped up surveillance of its workforce. Two articles in this section deal with new, highly sophisticated electronic cameras (some smaller than thimbles) and microphones that almost totally deny workers their privacy. Remaining articles disclose that telephones are often "bugged" and that everything an employee does on a computer, including E-mail messages received or sent out, can be called up by managers. Such heavy surveillance would also be the consequence of a federally mandated I.D. card which is discussed in the fifth article of this section. A special report by the ACLU, also included, reveals that electronic surveillance has increased markedly since 1990—and so has urine drug testing and genetic testing. While the constitution does not prohibit oversight of workers by managers, efforts to enact workplace privacy laws may help to insure that such oversight does not extend past the point of corporate need.

The question of privacy with respect to medical reports is the subject of Section Three. The section begins with a series of letters to the editor responding to a May 30, 1996 article by Dr. Jane Orient, in which Dr. Orient points out that an amendment to the Health Insurance Portability and Accountability Act, which became law in August 1996, could effectively eliminate the confidentiality of patient medical records as it requires the establishment of a centralized computer databank to hold those records. The following article offers a pro-and-con debate over the Medical Records Confidentiality Act. One writer, who supports the bill, argues that it will provide a uniform system for the handling of medical records, and will place sensible limits on access to them. A second writer, who opposes it, maintains that under its provisions companies could obtain medical records easily, and that the broad range of agencies and firms that could do so constitutes a serious breach of privacy.

Encapsulating the concerns of all those who are fearful that medical record confidentiality is not maintained, Christine Gorman, writing in *Time* magazine, provides examples of instances when patient confidentiality was clearly violated and the general reaction to those violations. The following article discusses the Human Genome Initiative, or the charting of all the genes which determine hereditary characteristics. This becomes a privacy issue when genes that predispose individuals to particular diseases are identified and that information becomes available to employers.

Cyberspace, and privacy concerns related to it, provide the subject of the fourth and final section of this anthology. As the opening article notes, Congress is currently interested in providing oversight to protect against marketers plundering E-mail for personal data. The next piece explores the implications of the National Information Infrastructure, or information superhighway, which, it is claimed, will eventually connect every home and business in the United States and the world to an evergrowing web of electronic services. Such a potential "global village," the author warns, could resemble life in Orwell's *1984*. Subsequent articles examine the Clinton administration's proposed "Clipper" chip program, designed to protect private electronic messages through an all-but-unbreakable encoding or encryption—with a "back door" provision enabling the government to break the code and unscramble messages when it is in the national interest. The final article concerns pornography on the Internet, and what can be done to circumvent it.

The editor is indebted to the authors and publishers who have granted permission to reprint the materials in this collection. Thanks are also due to the staff of Penfield Library, State University of New York, Oswego.

Robert Emmet Long
June 1997

I. Vanishing Privacy in the Information Society

Editor's Introduction

Articles in Section One have to do with the loss of privacy in an invasive electronic age. The opening piece, from *The Washington Monthly*, examines the options that the American public has to defend itself against intrusions upon its privacy. In the following article from *McCall's*, Jeffrey Rothfeder discusses the information that computer databases make available about American citizens who may believe they retain a high degree of privacy. Databases yield such information as a person's credit files, work history, driving records, health reports, bank balances, unlisted phone numbers, detailed phone records, criminal convictions, Social Security earnings, family statistics, and personal tastes and buying habits. The selling of such personal data by credit bureaus and "superbureaus" is now big business. In an article from *Newsweek*, Peter McGrath considers computerization and the availability of supposedly private information from users of the new online services. McGrath points out that anyone with $13,000 can buy "essentially the same search-and-retrieve facility as in all but the most advanced government and business systems."

The Economist notes that 80% of Americans fear they have "lost all control" over personal information as the postal service can sell one's new address, insurance companies can buy one's medical history, and employers can pry into the recesses of one's life with lie detector and psychological tests. Andrea Bernstein's piece from *Ms.* magazine takes up the question of the privacy rights of individuals considered to be undesirable or a potential threat to others—more specifically, sex offenders who have been released from prison and settle in a new neighborhood. If a released convict is a child molester, should the families in the new neighborhood be notified of his or her presence there? Such notification, under the so-called Megan's Law, is required in many communities and states, but is opposed by the ACLU.

Richard Spinello, in an article from *America*, describes a world where privacy is in short supply. According to Spinello, this lack of privacy can only undermine the freedom and dignity of Americans as well as pose a serious threat to their well-being and security. Spinello discusses the importance of privacy, the end of consumer, financial, and medical privacy, and the cumulative effect of this loss of privacy.

Privacy Wrongs[1]

Beverly Dennis is an Ohio grandmother and bona fide American consumer. Several years ago, she completed a questionnaire for the Metromail Corp., a direct marketing firm, in order to get free product samples. In her responses, she disclosed things like her income level, date of birth, the fact that she was divorced, her interest in physical fitness, and choice of "personal care" products, according to a lawsuit she is filing.

Dennis got more than free product samples. She got a "sexually graphic and threatening" letter from a convicted rapist in a Texas penitentiary. It turned out he knew quite a lot about Dennis, thanks to her questionnaire. He had written his highly personalized letter after being assigned the task of entering data from the questionnaire by a Metromail subcontractor. The use of inmates to answer 800-number calls, process consumer information, and even act as telemarketers, it seems, is widespread. "If it said [on the circular] it would be sent to a prison," Dennis later said in an interview, "I certainly wouldn't have filled it out."

Dennis is suing Metromail and the Texas criminal justice system for "outrageous disregard of public safety and dangerous invasion of privacy," among other things. It's hard not to feel that she has a point.

In fact, the manipulation of personal data that have been fed into the maw of the information society is, to cop an oft-used metaphor, like making sausage. If we really knew what was involved, we probably would want to have as little to do with the process as possible. The trouble is, we don't have that option. The relentless and systematic collection, compilation, and selling of personal information are built into the texture of everyday life. You may imagine that you can keep your distance from the vacuum-like data intakes by making shrewd choices about when, where, and to whom you disclose. But unless you're prepared to adopt a lifestyle like Theodore Kaczynski's, you're wrong.

Beverly Dennis, we trust, will bounce back from the nasty experience caused by the misappropriation of her data. But there's evidence that other types of misuse could be even more harmful.

With rising public anxiety about the victimization of children, for example, parents and other concerned adults are noticing how easy it is to get data that could be put to sinister use. To dramatize the point, a Los Angeles television reporter recently purchased from Metromail a list of 5,500 children, with their family names and addresses. Not to make the exercise too subtle, the reporter placed the order in the name of Richard Allen Davis, the

> *"The use of inmates to...act as telemarketers, it seems, is widespread."*

[1] Article by James B. Rule, editor of *Dissent* with Lawrence Hunter, a computer scientist at the National Institute of Health, from *The Washington Monthly* 28:17-20 N '96. Copyright © 1996 The Washington Monthly Company, Washington, D.C. Reprinted with permission.

man convicted for abducting, sexually assaulting, and murdering 12-year-old Polly Klaas.

It's hard to say precisely where these particular data originated. We do know that lists like this are compiled from such sources as the "birthday clubs" that retailers encourage parents to enroll their kids in, subscription lists for children's magazines, and toy store discount cards. What is almost certain is that whoever provided the information did not realize he or she was helping to feed a commercial data bank.

The most alarming uses of personal data often involve the least obtrusive forms of collection. Take getting a prescription filled. Increasingly, this involves feeding the patients' and physicians' names, along with other identifying data on the people and drugs involved, into a computer. Sometimes the acknowledged purpose of the data entry is to determine whether the charges are covered by insurance. In some places, laws require prescription data to be fed into government systems aimed at curbing prescription drug abuse. But whatever the ostensible purposes, people lose control over their information once it enters the data stream.

"In some places, laws require prescription data to be fed into government systems aimed at curbing prescription drug abuse."

Often pharmacists sell information to "switchers"—operations that find buyers for such data. Some switchers, for example, collate information on users of specific drugs for sale to manufacturers of over-the-counter companion drugs. Then manufacturers direct advertising appeals to the targeted patients. Are these practices beneficial to patients? Conceivably, if the companion drug helps. Can they be dangerous? Quite possibly, for those who use the new medication without seeking medical advice from their own physicians.

But for most Americans, the issue here is probably not whether these practices are medically beneficial. It is that people whose data are appropriated in these ways have no say in what happens to their information. Indeed, it's not even legally theirs. Patients may have thought that their prescriptions were a matter between themselves and their pharmacists, but that idea is going the way of vinyl records. There is just too much demand for personal information, and there are too many sophisticated techniques for getting it.

Some may consider this the inevitable by-product of living in an information age. But these leaks can lead to authentic tragedies. John Doe, an AIDS sufferer, was a middle-level manager of the Southeastern Pennsylvania Transportation Authority (SEPTA). He had disclosed his condition only to his immediate superior at SEPTA, someone he trusted. But then other managers at the organization noted that Doe's charges on the employer-backed prescription plan were unusually high and had his account audited. The investigation showed that Doe had been getting prescriptions for Retrovir, an anti-AIDS drug.

The result for Doe was stigmatization at work over matters that he had every right to keep to himself. Doe had maybe a year left in his work life, his attorney Clifford Boardman told *Newsday*, and every day was important to him. This disclosure took away his peace of mind. A federal jury awarded Doe $125,000, but the verdict was overturned on appeal. "We hold that a self insured employer's need for access to employee prescription records outweighs an employee's interest in keeping his prescription drug purchases confidential," the U.S. Circuit Court of Appeals concluded.

Businesses are increasingly realizing there's a gold mine in personal data. Fortunes await those who can devise slick ways for distinguishing who should receive consumer credit, and on what terms; or for identifying profitable customers for insurance companies; or for specifying the best targets for marketing campaigns. These incentives have led to the growth of vast industries that depend on personal information as the essential raw material.

The sources for the data are all but endless, and often unobtrusive. Every call to an 800 number is apt to disclose the caller's phone number, giving resourceful data collectors access to the caller's name and address. One phone company recently created an electronic system that flashes information about the social characteristics of the caller's neighborhood. Internet transactions and website visits also may enable data collectors to infer the caller's identity. Every product coupon submitted for a rebate, every warranty slip filed with a manufacturer, every credit card sale—almost any identifiable fact about an American consumer—may provide grist for the commercial information mills.

Not all the sources are commercial enterprises. Charities, magazines, hospitals, and countless other not-for-profit organizations sell their data. Activist groups from right to left often sell lists of their supporters or trade them with other organizations. The U.S. Postal Service now routinely releases customers' change-of-address information—typically without their knowledge—to businesses who want it.

State motor vehicle registrars have long realized that records they compile—under legal compulsion—of accidents, driving infractions, and the like are valuable to insurance companies. Many states turn a pretty penny releasing driver data to insurance companies and the organizations that serve them. It makes financial sense; millions of requests per year at several dollars apiece help offset many a state budget deficit.

"Every call to an 800 number is apt to disclose the caller's phone number..."

Record Sales

A typical mailing list company trumpets the availability of information on "83 million families, selectable by income, age, credit card use, mail-order buying, number (and age) of children, type of automobile, type of home..." For an additional price, the same broker will provide "ethnic name selection," guessing the ethnicity of those in their databases by statistical analysis of names. Customers may wish to select, for example, names and phone numbers of all the black accountants in Washington, D.C., or contributors to gay charities, or purchasers of products for incontinence.

The ability to deal with vast numbers of individuals, while still attending to the fine detail of individual cases, yields stunning capabilities. And it's most alarming with medical data. The rise of third-party payment for medical needs and intense competition—among insurers, employers, and other businesses—to avoid people who might develop costly diseases have fueled ferocious appetites for personal data.

In a case reported recently in *Time*, for example, a banker serving on a state health commission pulled a list of cancer patients in his area, determined which ones had loans with his bank, then called in the loans. And as with the AIDS sufferer mentioned earlier, prescription and other medical records are increasingly accessible to companies carrying medical insurance for their staffs. This dual role—employer and provider of medical insurance—tends inexorably to bring data together from relationships most of us would like to see hermetically walled off from one another.

In April 1996, *Newsday* reporter John Riley told the story of Veronica, a patient whose psychotherapy for depression was covered by her employer. Like many in the same situation, Veronica was alarmed to learn that, to extend the treatment, her therapist had to provide details of her problems to the managed care company paying the bills. Routinely, Riley writes, "doctors, patients and pharmacists...must feed patient information up the system's food chain to insurers who may, in turn, share it with each other, with employers and with information vendors in a virtually unregulated process."

This is not to say the manipulation of personal data has no advantages. We can be offered useful products and services we would otherwise miss. But what is at stake are the legal and social arrangements that will shape technological changes now in course. The current framework simply doesn't reflect the realities of a world where personal information has become the essential raw material for several major industries.

Of course, there are some important protections for personal information. The Privacy Act of 1974, which gave individuals access to data held by government agencies and allowed them to challenge its accuracy, was a positive step. If this law has a salient flaw, it is its failure in practice to achieve what was a key element of its original intent—to prevent data collected for one purpose from being used for other purposes that may not suit the interests of the provider.

Nothing so comprehensive as the Privacy Act exists for private-sector data. Coverage is piecemeal and chaotic. The occasional checks on appropriation of personal data—such as the right to review your credit record to make sure it's accurate—found in one sector are lacking elsewhere. As medical privacy specialist Sheri Alpert has commented, one's choices of video rentals are better protected under current American law than one's medical records. Under the "Bork law," passed after that judge's video rental choices were revealed during his Supreme Court confirmation hearings, video customers have the right to "opt out" from disclosure. In most other commercial areas (most medical contexts included) personal data belong to whoever has possession of them. Thus many hospitals, like the pharmacies we mentioned earlier, sell personal data from their records.

Americans are certainly realizing their privacy is increasingly at risk. In September, the database firm Lexis-Nexis found itself in the midst of a firestorm of public complaint after people discovered the firm was selling access to individuals' data—Social Security numbers, maiden names, addresses, and the like. Librarian Robert Gitlin told the *Los Angeles Times*, "It's private information that I don't want released without any opportunity to consent."

Though worsening, this problem is not new. For years, many have sought omnibus legislation to establish a blanket right to privacy. They have failed, though, because privacy is a contested value; the interest in protecting personal data often collides with other legitimate interests. My desire to keep my medical history to myself, for example, will always be at odds with the interests of insurers in auditing the care I receive. Any reasonable policy would give both privacy and "right-to-know" interests their due.

"Americans are certainly realizing their privacy is increasingly at risk."

Righting the Wrong

That's why we propose the creation of personal property rights that would supersede the commercial exploitation of personal information. Without express authorization from the subject, no personal data could be sold or traded from any file for any commercial purpose. Release of credit card data to credit reporting agencies, "switching" of prescription information for marketing purposes, or the resale of records from mail order firms to direct marketing firms would all be prohibited—unless the release of such data was explicitly authorized by the individual in question.

The immediate result of such a principle would be a new—and entirely healthy—set of choices and tensions. People would have to take careful stock of their interests in the use of their data, weighing privacy interests against other considerations. Imagine, for example, a consumer put off by a credit bureau's collection of information on her retail accounts, or unable to resolve a dispute with the credit bureau over her records. She could choose to prevent the release of further data to credit bureaus, or to prevent the current bureau from selling further reports. The bureau might then have the right to report that the record was sealed at the consumer's request, but no more.

Of course, consumers would have to weigh the consequences of their decisions—forgoing the benefits of having a credit record, or risking that creditors would choose not to do business with them or would charge them a higher rate of interest. Similarly, those denying their medical histories to insurance reporting firms might well find access to some forms of insurance blocked, or the costs of coverage raised. Because many consumers would probably choose to reap the benefits of releasing their information, commerce would not come grinding to a halt. But this system would place the onus of decision squarely where it belongs—on the individual who provides the data.

The information industry would then have incentives to make their activities acceptable to the people whose information they take, instead of just collecting it without their knowledge or permission. The credit reporting industry would have to sell its services to the public—presumably by promising more accurate, open reporting practices and by calling attention to the benefits of having an active and complete credit record. Direct marketers would have to convince the public that their attentions were, on balance, an advantage to the customer. Businesses would need to convince customers that the sale of their information really worked to their advantage—if not, customers would simply refuse their permission for release.

One end result of this new right would be a decrease in the quantity of privacy-invading experiences, from junk telephone calls to unwanted appropriations of medical information, and a rise in their quality—that is, the potential they will actually benefit the individual concerned.

Some legislative straws in the wind suggest that public opinion may now be open to a right like the one proposed here. GOP Congressman Bob Franks has proposed a bill to require parental consent before children's data can be commercialized. New Jersey state Sen. Richard Codey last February introduced a bill barring companies from renting or selling consumer names "without prior written or electronic consent" from the party concerned. About the same time, the Minnesota legislature was considering a similar bill applying to on-line service companies.

The courts are also starting to address the problem. In a case against Radio Shack, Robert Beken won $1,000 in damages for misuse of his personal data. Beken had written a contract on the back of his check to the electronics chain, committing them not to place him on the store's mailing list or send him any advertisements or mailings. The court rejected Radio Shack's defense that the clerk accepting the check had no authority to enter into such a contract with Beken.

But we believe that court decisions or piecemeal legislation will never provide the protection that would be afforded by a comprehensive right. The right we propose would not categorically block any of the useful forms of data exchange underlying today's information society. Nor would it prevent any organization from maintaining its own files on clients or customers—provided that the data involved were provided by, or with the consent of, those concerned. It would simply require their permission before their data could be released.

Who could take exception to the institution of personal data rights? Only the vast industries that now appropriate personal data for free. Information-collecting industries have often sought immunity from privacy-protecting legislation on freedom of expression grounds. But it hardly makes sense to identify the same value in "commercial speech" as in expression of opinion on public affairs, which would still be protected. Nothing proposed here, for example, should detract from the right of journalists or others to obtain personal data on public figures for news stories or other forms of public discussion.

This measure wouldn't solve all the sticky policy dilemmas associated with privacy protection. Some personal data no doubt should never be marketed for commercial use—those on children, for example, or individuals' DNA profiles. But establishing a general property right in personal data would create a potent new weapon for ordinary Americans to defend themselves against pressures on their privacy. With the information age hitting high gear in the 1990s, there's only so much time to get the genie back in the bottle. Otherwise, we will just have to adjust to living in see-through houses on the information highway.

Dangerous Things Strangers Know About You[2]

It was one of the most alarming phone conversations Karen Hochman of New York City had ever had. A long-distance company had called to convince her to switch carriers. But Hochman wasn't interested. "I told him that I didn't make many out-of-town calls, but thanks anyway."

"I'm surprised to hear you say that," the salesman interjected. "I see from your phone records that you frequently call New Jersey, Delaware and Connecticut." Hochman was shocked and scared by the salesman's invasion of her privacy. "How the hell did you get hold of my phone records?" she asked and then threatened legal action. The salesman quickly hung up.

"The types of data available are mind-boggling..."

"If strangers are able to find out the numbers I call, what else could they find out about me?" wondered Hochman.

A lot, as it turns out. With computers on most office desktops and in many homes, and with huge databases able to feed these machines, we now live in a world where personal data is big business—bought and sold with relative ease. The types of data available are mind-boggling: credit files, work history, driving records, health reports, bank balances, nonpublished phone numbers, phone records, criminal convictions, Social Security earnings, family makeup, personal tastes and buying habits.

Enterprising marketers, and most anyone with a computer and the required fee, can purchase general information from original sources, such as credit or government agencies. And though they won't sell the most sensitive information to just anyone, there are dozens of information resellers, known as superbureaus, that often will.

The worst thing about this information blitzkrieg is that—even though errors abound—what's said about us by computers is usually considered accurate, and significant decisions are made based on this information. Often those affected are unaware of the process and are given no chance to offer explanations.

For example, insurers use computerized data to decide who should get life, disability and medical coverage—and who should be denied it. Employers make hiring decisions based on computer-compiled reports. Junk mailers and telemarketers make billions of sales pitches a year using computer profiles. Those who have access to these files could share this private information, causing damage that can range from embarrassment to ruined reputations. And increasingly criminals use databases to take on the identity of others and get car loans, mortgages, credit cards

---

[2] Article by Jeffrey Rothfeder, author and editor, from *McCall's* 121:88+ Ja '94. Copyright © 1994 Jeffrey Rothfeder. Reprinted with permission.

and a lot more in those people's names.

Don't expect the law to shield you. There's no federal legisla
tion protecting medical, telephone, employment, insurance and
bank records—some of our most sensitive data. And the few privacy laws on the books—like the 1970 Fair Credit Reporting Act
or the 1974 Privacy Act—are outmoded vestiges of the precom-
puter age. Some state statutes exist, but they're hard to enforce.

If you think you're careful about giving out personal information, consider this: There are few areas of our lives not prey to
this sprawling information net. Each time you book a flight, your
name, address, credit-card number and where and when you're
going are entered into the airline's reservation computers. This
data is sold to rental car companies, travel agents and others.

Warranty cards are another key source of information for marketers, as most people willingly fill in such data as their family
size, where they shop, even what they earn.

Here, we spotlight some of the most shocking things strangers
know about you—and how you can help protect yourself.

1. What You Earn, What You Owe

"Superbureaus subscribe to the credit bureaus and sell credit reports via computer..."

THE PROBLEM: The nation's three biggest credit bureaus—TRW,
Equifax and Trans Union—store 500 million records on more
than 160 million people. The financial data in their files include:
employment and salary histories; credit-card numbers, transactions and balances; mortgage records; bankruptcies; and tax
liens.

The credit bureaus constantly comb bank, credit-card and
other records for unusual signs—for instance, late payments, an
increase in salary, a higher mortgage. Then, without permission,
they share these tidbits with banks, retailers and marketers.
Superbureaus subscribe to the credit bureaus and sell credit
reports via computer to virtually anyone who pays the sign-up
fee, from $100 to $500, plus $20 to $50 extra for each specific
report.

For example, evangelist Oral Roberts once sent out a letter that
read, "I am your partner and your friend.... It's time for you to
get out from under a load of debt.... If you could just suddenly
receive a big lump sum of money, all your problems would be
over.... I have a miraculous answer, direct from the throne of
God to your home." The solution: Send $100 to Roberts and he
would intercede with God.

How did Roberts know the recipient was in a bind? It wasn't
divine intervention, just computers. Roberts bought a list of people who were at least 60 days late on their credit-card bills.

HOW IT AFFECTS YOU: Marketers use credit-bureau data for
targeted junk-mail campaigns—so your mailbox may be flooded
with unwanted solicitations. Creditors use credit-bureau tips to
unfairly shut off the accounts of people whose general solvency
appears to be slipping—even if they are still paying their bills on

time—to avoid getting stiffed down the road. It's legal for them to do this because having a credit card is a privilege, not a right. Criminals access credit data to steal money using the identity of others.

PRIVACY PRECAUTION: Get your credit report once a year from each credit bureau to look for inaccuracies, transactions you haven't made and the names of people who have accessed it. You can investigate people or companies that have obtained your report and perhaps stave off embezzlement or fraud. Call TRW at 800-682-7654 (they offer one free report a year) and Equifax at 800-685-1111 ($8). Write to Trans Union, PO Box 7000, North Olmsted, OH 44070 (include $8 and your Social Security number, previous address and any previous name).

"There are statutes in two dozen states that allow for the release of medical records..."

To stop receiving junk mail, write to Direct Marketing Association, Mail Preference Service, PO Box 3861, New York, NY 10163.

To delete your name from credit bureaus' marketing lists, contact Consumer Relations, TRW Target Marketing Services, 901 N. International Pkwy., Richardson, TX 75081; and Trans Union Corp., Transmark Div., Name Removal Option, 555 W. Adams St., Chicago, IL 60661. To get your name off lists sold by your credit-card companies, contact them directly.

2. What Only Your Doctor, And You, Should Know

THE PROBLEM: Medical records aren't private. The Medical Information Bureau (MIB), an insurance consortium, collects physician and hospital records on millions of Americans and Canadians. No federal laws restrict when and to whom a medical record can be revealed. There are statutes in two dozen states that allow for the release of medical records only with a patient's approval; but people give their consent almost every time they sign an application for insurance, loans, credit or employment. In fine print these applications usually state that a background check, including looking at an MIB file, may be conducted. Many of these forms have no expiration date, so they can be used to access your medical records at any time.

HOW IT AFFECTS YOU: The information contained in your medical profile—accurate or not—can impact your reputation, employment, insurance and licenses.

PRIVACY PRECAUTION: You can ask your doctor not to give out information unless you approve. Limit blanket medical-record release forms by writing in that your okay is only for the specific purpose of the application. Though it can be expensive, some employees pay for their drug- or alcohol abuse treatments and programs to keep their employer from finding out. For a free copy of your MIB file, call 617-426-3660.

3. How Much You've Saved

THE PROBLEM: By law federal agencies—except criminal authorities like the FBI—can't look at your bank records without a warrant or your consent. But, inexplicably, individual private companies can, though most banks have ethics rules that make this data private.

But even with those ethics rules, sources inside a bank, usually low-level clerks, do secretly access information via the computer on their desk.

New technology has made privacy matters even worse. Transactions at automatic-teller machines (ATMs) are accessed electronically by computer hackers who monitor ATM activity to take down personal identification numbers and account data.

"Deposit slips are a clue to salary and bonuses..."

HOW IT AFFECTS YOU: Some of the biggest buyers of bank-account data are estranged spouses, angry business partners and embezzlers. A lot can be gleaned from these files, beyond account balance: Deposit slips are a clue to salary and bonuses; what checks are used for indicates taste and lifestyle; and whom checks are made out to provides names of friends, associates and business contacts such as brokers. Direct marketers also use this data for mail- or telephone-based sales campaigns. Even though banks usually don't sell information on individuals, some openly sell this data in list form; for example, as a list of customers who make a certain income.

PRIVACY PRECAUTION: Ask if your bank would agree in writing to notify you when someone asks to access your records. Don't fill in memo lines on checks or write your Social Security, telephone, driver's license or credit card numbers on checks. Examine ATM receipts to make sure the balance is correct; if it's not, someone may be monitoring your ATM activity and embezzling money from your account.

4. Whom You Call

THE PROBLEM: Virtually every 800 or 900 number has caller ID attached to it. So when you call, you're giving away your identity.

HOW IT AFFECTS YOU: Mostly this is used to create lists—containing your phone number, name and address—that are sold to marketers.

PRIVACY PRECAUTION: If you don't want to get on mailing lists, avoid calling these numbers. Use caller-ID blocking if it's available in your area. Don't give out personal information—such as Social Security or credit-card numbers—to anybody on the phone, unless you initiated the business transaction.

Info 'Snooper-Highway'[3]

Every keystroke can be monitored. And the computers never forget. Two cautions for the Information Age.

Of all the effects of high-speed global data networks, none seems quite as insidious as the noose they draw around traditional American notions of personal privacy. Just ask the members of the WELL, a small but cutting-edge online service based in Sausalito, Calif. Last week they were alarmed to learn that Kevin Mitnick, a notorious hacker in North Carolina, allegedly had not only broken into the service's computers and begun reading their electronic mail but also used the WELL as a screen behind which he was able to launch anonymous attacks on networks throughout the Internet. Before being arrested, he even taunted WELL administrators by stashing stolen computer files on one of their servers, in a directory entitled "Computers, Freedom and Privacy."

"Anyone who opened a bank account was leaving electronic traces of his or her house payments..."

It was a bracing reminder of the fragility of privacy on what is fast becoming known as the "information snooper-highway." "With new online services, we're all excited that this is going to be our window on the world, movies, consumer services, for talking with our friends," says Marc Rotenberg, director of the Washington-based Electronic Privacy Information Center. "The reality is that this may be a window looking *in*."

Intimate details: Concern about computers and privacy dates back to the 1960s, when governments first began to store their files on the room-filling machines then in use. As computerized record-keeping spread to the private sector, the machines became repositories for the most intimate details of people's lives. Anyone who opened a bank account was leaving electronic traces of his or her house payments, buying habits, visits to the doctor. Telephone service created trails leading to families and friends. Even a social-security number was a potential liability: with it, a dedicated sleuth could pry the holder's tax returns loose from government computers.

Since then, invading privacy has become steadily easier, almost as a corollary of Moore's Law, a Silicon Valley maxim that computer power doubles every two years. More and more personal data take digital form. Driver's-license numbers provide electronic links to the licensee's physical characteristics and driving record. Credit cards and automated-teller-machine cards make financial records even more accessible. At the same time, computers themselves operate at speeds that were unthinkable a few years ago: personal computers running Intel's Pentium chip are more than 300 times faster than machines with the same compa-

---

[3] Article by Peter McGrath, staffwriter, from *Newsweek* 125:60-61 F 27 '95. Copyright © 1995 Newsweek, Inc. Reprinted with permission.

ny's first-generation PC chip, the 8086. Today, anyone with $3,000 can buy essentially the same search-and-retrieve facility as in all but the most advanced government and business systems.

As a result, surveillance is now a brokerage business. Where once this was the domain of experts in such arts as wiretapping, the barriers to entry have been lowered. Consider Sandy Martin, a private investigator in Wilmette, Ill., who was asked last year to track down an elderly man based on nothing but his name. The client was the man's daughter, a New Jersey woman anxious to know if the father she had never met was a carrier of a blood disorder. Martin collated nine database searches, all of them legal., to locate a man in Florida with the right name and the right approximate age, 84. A phone call confirmed that he was the woman's father. The entire search took four days from a desktop computer and cost the client $1,500. Martin says the pre-PC way would have consumed two months and more than $10,000. As computer power increases, so does the information available. Commercial online services routinely ask members to submit personal profiles along with their credit-card numbers. These might include not only names and addresses but hobbies—items that could be used to create mailing lists of great value to advertisers and marketers. The services typically check members' computer hard drives every time they log on, the purpose is to determine any need for software updates, but the scan can also surreptitiously record valuable information about the way members have configured their machines and what software they use. Until customer protests forced it to back down, a Beaverton, Ore.-based company called Central Point Software did just that, as part of registering its PC Tools for Windows.

Every online keystroke leaves its fingerprint on the service's central computers. Over time, system operators could build detailed profiles of members based on their electronic mail, the Internet newsgroups they subscribe to, the kinds of software they download. Such profiles could then be sold to telemarketers or others using online services to send demographically targeted commercial messages. These records are vulnerable to penetration from outside, too. Last month, 28 Harvard students were mortified to learn that the campus newspaper, the *Crimson*, had identified them as consumers of pornography simply by tracking their Internet activities through the university's network.

In the end, we compromise ourselves. We leave traces of our lives in databases everywhere. Computers are built to recognize patterns, to find coherence in individually insignificant details. If we then lose our privacy, it's because we volunteered.

"The services typically check members' computer hard drives every time they log on..."

Newsweek poll:

- 85% are concerned about pornography being too available to young people through the Internet
- 80% are concerned about being harassed by "virtual stalking" through unwanted messages on the Internet
- 76% are concerned about being harassed by real stalking from someone they first meet on the Internet

We Know You're Reading This[4]

A day in the life of an ordinary American: he drives to the office, toils at a computer, browses in shops at lunchtime, then picks up some bread and a video on the way home, where a pile of junk mail and a doctor's bill await him. At every stop along the way, his doings can be watched, monitored, tabulated and sold.

Americans think they have a right to privacy. After all, in 1965 the Supreme Court famously found such a right in the "penumbras" and "emanations" of the American constitution. Despite this, they have lost control over who knows what about them. The chief culprit is not so much Big Brother as lots of little brothers, all gossiping with each other over computer networks. But Big Brother is doing his bit: in the struggle against crime, terrorism, deadbeat parents, illegal immigrants and even traffic jams, the government keeps an ever-closer eye on more and more of its citizens.

On a typical day, for example, our hero's driving route may be tracked by an intelligent traffic system. At work, his employer can legally listen in to his business conversations on the telephone, and tap into his computer, e-mail or voice-mail. At the shopping centre, the ubiquitous closed-circuit camera may soon be smart enough to seek him out personally. His clothes shop is allowed to put peepholes in the fitting-rooms, some have hidden microphones, too. The grocery stores information about him if he is a member of its "buyers' club".

If he uses his credit card, not only does the card company keep tabs on when, where and what he buys, it may sell that knowledge to eager merchants. A purchase of outdoor furniture means that brochures hawking barbecue grills, lawn seed and funny aprons are likely to follow: hence the junk mail piled on his doorstep. The doctors' bills and other sorts of medical information are better guarded; but in many American states trade in private medical records is perfectly legal. (In 22 states, on the other hand, patients lack the right to see their medical files.) If he calls a toll-free 800 number or a pay-per-minute 900 number, the other end can identify his telephone number—even if it is unlisted—and sell it.

And if he decides to give up the rat race and become a Texan cowboy, the postal service will sell his new address to anyone who asks. His new employer can get his medical history from the insurance company, and his credit history from a credit bureau. Just to be hired, he may have to take a drug test, a lie-detector test (though this is now limited to certain fields), and a psychological test. He may have to tell his employer which prescription

"A purchase of outdoor furniture means that brochures hawking barbecue grills, lawn seed and funny aprons are likely to follow..."

---

[4] Article by staffwriter from *The Economist* 338:27-28 F 10 '96. Copyright © 1996 The Economist Newspaper Group, Inc. Reprinted with permission. Further reproduction prohibited.

drugs he takes and whether he has smoked in the past year.

His choice of videos, at least, is protected: to tell which films he hires is illegal. But that is not much comfort in a world where legal databases match addresses with unlisted telephone numbers, and illegal ones do a brisk trade in bank, stock and tax information. With the right software, any aspiring Sherlock can build up a large file on most Americans, including education, previous addresses, physical description, telephone bills, hobbies, and more. The armchair detective can even hire someone to do it for him: given a telephone number, at least one service will cull a credit database and supply an address, demographic information and buying preferences.

Did someone say "privacy"? Hush. Marketing and consumer-products firms like to know who buys what—and where and when and how. Law-enforcement officials, too, are pleased to have new and better ways to snoop, often in response to pressures from the public. For example, the State Directory of New Hires, a pilot programme operating in five states, is intended to prevent illegal immigrants from working. Employers who hire a worker must contact the federal government, which checks to ensure that the new bloke has his papers. The system involves the feds in every decision to hire, which is a troubling precedent; and of course it will make mistakes.

The state of Maryland requires every hospital visit to be logged into a database; the idea is that by gathering such information, health and administration costs may be cut. But this compromises the once-sacrosanct principle that used to shield doctor-patient communications from public view.

Two cases burning up the Internet show the extent to which technology has become the front line in the battles over privacy. In one case, a law passed last year required telephone companies to design their equipment to allow for wiretaps. In the other, the federal government tried to enforce use of the "Clipper chip", a device which would ensure that it could read all encrypted messages.

Officials argued that in both cases the status quo—access to private communications upon a court order—was just being extended. Furious cybercitizens disagreed. "Trusting the government with your privacy", snorted Wired magazine, "is like having a Peeping Tom install your window blinds." Officialdom backed off on the Clipper chip because it couldn't make people buy it, but it is now pushing a related scheme that would allow a "trusted third party", such as a company or a nonprofit group, to keep the keys to private codes on behalf of the government.

Selling Secrets, and Secrecy

The conflict is a classic one: between individual rights and the public good, between the demands of law-enforcement and the preservation of a private sphere. To resolve it, a principle is needed. There used to be one: data could not be gathered or used for another purpose without the consent of the person concerned. In these days of multilinked databases, that principle is history.

Today, the presumed right to privacy is giving way to the right to protect one's privacy. Although few realize it, Americans are generally able to see the files kept on them, to correct mistakes, block disclosure (sometimes, at least) and to learn where information has gone. Consumers have the right to check their credit reports and to insist on giving permission before they are released. Junk-mail recipients can write to the Direct Marketing Association to be placed on the "delete" list (but companies not part of the association must be contacted directly).

All well and good. But tracking down dozens of information-gatherers—government agencies, department stores, mail-order companies and so on—is no easy task, and it is not always possible to know which databases you are in, anyway. (One, which retailers like to consult, lists former salesmen suspected of theft; names can be added without telling the persons concerned.)

Given all this, it is not unreasonable that 80% of Americans tell pollsters they worry that they have "lost all control" over personal information. But at the same time they are extraordinarily willing to fill out warranty cards, questionnaires and impertinent surveys. In short, Americans love information, but they have not figured out how they want to control access to it.

"Congress and many states have passed the odd law to answer specific privacy complaints..."

In response, Congress and many states have passed the odd law to answer specific privacy complaints: the rule against disclosing videos, for example, and limits on the disclosure of driving records. Europe passed a comprehensive set of data protection guidelines in October. The last such federal legislation in America dates back to the Privacy Act of 1974.

Much of the law on privacy is therefore being made in vintage American style—the courts are making it up as they go along. One case to watch is in Virginia, where the law forbids the use of anyone's likeness for commercial purposes without his consent. On this basis, a subscriber is suing *U.S. News & World Report*, an American weekly, for selling his name and address—which, he claims, are forms of his likeness.

Peeping Sam, Look to Discreet Europe

There are other pressures for change. Under the European directive, transfer of sensitive information to countries with inadequate privacy laws would not be allowed. If America's current muddle does not pass muster, business could be cut off from information from Europe—a powerful incentive to fix what's broke.

And technology itself may provide a partial answer. All-but-foolproof encryption technology is freely available over the Internet and will not go away no matter how much Uncle Sam wishes it would. A Dutch firm, Digicash, has developed e-cash, which allows customers to buy goods over the Internet directly and anonymously. Digicash has also developed a smart card—

compatible with Eurocard, Visa and Mastercard—that makes payment anonymous.

It is in the computer industry's interest to sort the issues out. Computer networks will not fulfill their commercial potential if consumers worry that their credit-card security and personal privacy will be snagged in the Internet. Already, certain sites on the Internet make an explicit commitment to privacy. Confidentiality, like information, is attractive to customers—and thus should be marketable. Attention, Kmart shoppers: privacy for sale, aisle nine.

Should You Be Told That Your Neighbor Is a Sex Offender?[5]

July 29, 1994, had been a scorcher in Hamilton Township, New Jersey. But by the time seven-year-old Megan Kanka had finished eating dinner with her family, the day had cooled. As she did most evenings after supper, Megan, a smiling, blond-haired child, crossed their quiet street to play with a friend. "She'd done this hundreds of times," says Megan's mother, Maureen Kanka. But this time, Megan never returned.

According to prosecutors, the man who lived across the street, Jesse Timmendequas, a twice-convicted sex offender, lured Megan into his home with the promise of showing her his puppy. But instead, prosecutors argued at his bail hearing, Timmendequas strangled Megan with a belt, then anally and vaginally penetrated her. To cover up the crime, they said, Timmendequas snuck her body out of the house in a toy box. Then he allegedly washed down his steps, the box, and his truck with ammonia when he heard that the police were checking the neighborhood with dogs. Later he offered to help neighbors distribute flyers about the missing girl. Within days, Timmendequas was arrested for Megan's murder; he is currently in jail awaiting trial.

"Decisions about who poses a risk to society fall to a panel of prosecutors..."

Megan's death hit a raw nerve. With crime-fighting fever infecting the nation, a groundswell of support sprang up in New Jersey for what has come to be known as "Megan's Law." The state legislation mandates that authorities notify residents—by distributing flyers, alerting local organizations, and door-to-door canvassing—when sex offenders who are at high risk of reoffense move into their neighborhoods. Decisions about who poses a risk to society fall to a panel of prosecutors who consider, among other factors, whether the offender received counseling, whether the original crime involved a weapon, whether it resulted in serious bodily harm, and whether the offender will be supervised by a parole officer. Just three months after Megan's death, New Jersey Governor Christine Todd Whitman signed the proposed legislation into law.

It had been rushed through the state legislature with virtually no debate. There are now 28 states with some form of community notification, although Megan's Law goes further than most; whereas other states make information about released offenders available to the public, New Jersey is the first state to require authorities to alert communities. A majority of these new

---

[5] Article by Andrea Bernstein, New York City-based writer and talk show host, from *Ms.* 6:24-26 N/D '95. Copyright © 1995 *Ms.* Magazine. Reprinted with permission.

statutes cover all types of sex offenders, not just child molesters. And Representative Dick Zimmer (R.-N.J.) has introduced a measure in the House that would require every state to enact a community notification law.

Will these measures reduce the recurrence of sex crimes—or do they create the illusion of public safety while putting individual rights at risk? Community notification proponents have powerful allies: most lawmakers, governors, and the Clinton administration. Lining up against such legislation are the American Civil Liberties Union (ACLU) and a host of psychologists and criminal justice experts. But for the most part, the sweeping changes affecting sex crimes laws have so far taken place with little comment from women's groups. Some feminists say they're swamped by the wholesale assault on welfare and affirmative action, and simply haven't had time to focus on the issue; those who have are divided.

"A 1989 Justice Department study...found that 32 percent of burglars, for example, were rearrested for burglary within the first three years of their release..."

The central premise of community notification laws is that sex offenders are much more likely than other criminals to reoffend. Thus, the theory goes, by knowing who potential reoffenders are, the public can protect itself. Megan's Law advocates cite studies like one conducted in Washington State, which found that 13 percent of adult offenders and 12 percent of juvenile offenders were rearrested for sex crimes within seven years. Within 15 years, a California study shows, almost 20 percent of adult sex offenders commit another sex crime.

But opponents of community notification argue that sex offenders' recidivism rates are actually lower than those of other criminals. A 1989 Justice Department study, which had the largest sample size of any study of released criminals to date, found that 32 percent of burglars, for example, were rearrested for burglary within the first three years of their release—compared to 8 percent of rapists rearrested for rape. Megan's Law defenders counter that tracking arrest records doesn't show the whole picture because sex crimes are reported far less than other crimes.

Some opponents of notification fear that, far from offering women and children greater protection, it could actually put them at greater risk—by making offenders even more determined to avoid arrest. The attitude would be, "If you kill the witness, maybe you'll get away with it," says Nathaniel Pallone, Rutgers University Professor of Psychology and Criminal Justice. Other opponents, like the ACLU, say that notification laws run roughshod over sex offenders' civil rights, such as the right to due process, privacy, and equal protection, and provisions against after-the-fact and cruel and unusual punishment.

Topping the ACLU's list of concerns is that community notification can lead to vigilantism. That's what happened in Washington State the day convicted child rapist Joseph Gallardo was released from prison—his Lynnwood home was burned to the ground. But notification proponents say that only a small fraction of identified offenders have been harassed. And some note the possible deterrent effect of community outrage: "If the molesters are afraid the community will know about their criminal acts, then maybe they'd better not commit criminal acts against children. They should have thought of that in the first place," says feminist attorney Gloria Allred, who is based in Los Angeles. "I'm more concerned about the wrongs committed against children than the rights of child molesters."

Other feminists, like Columbia University law professor Patricia Williams, are unsettled by notification laws. "Like so many movements that are sweeping the country, it looks like theatrics as opposed to what works," she says, adding that she's concerned that "Megan's Law adds a punishment on top of sentence already served." But the courts don't see it that way. The constitutional rights to privacy, to equal protection, and to freedom from cruel and unusual punishment have not been found to preclude notification laws.

Do sex-offender notification laws achieve their stated purpose of preventing repeat offenses? Opponents like sex-offender researcher Robert Prentky, of Philadelphia's Joseph J. Peters Institute, say they provide a false sense of security: "If someone is destined to reoffend, it's obvious that all they will do is get in a car and drive to an adjoining community. If neighbors on the street know you, you can still reoffend in the next town or the next state." Critics also note that only a tiny percentage of child sex offenders fit the stereotype of the skulking stranger haunting a playground. "Such legislation perpetuates the notion that a child molester is an invader rather than someone among you. But most molestation takes place within known circles," says Williams.

Nevertheless, says feminist Linda Hirshman, a professor at Chicago-Kent School of Law, notification can reduce the odds of being sexually assaulted. "If you had a picture, at least you could show the picture and say don't go near this man." It would have made all the difference for Megan, says her mother. "In Megan's eyes, [the accused murderer] was the neighbor. The kids saw him walking the dog. She had no reason to fear him."

When it comes to protecting women, notification laws might help but "aren't nearly enough," says Alice Vachss, the former Chief of the Special Victims Bureau of the Queens District Attorney's Office in New York. "People who think notification laws are a solution have been sold a bill of goods by politicians. The real problem is that we still choose what rapists we're going to go after based on whether we like the victim, whether we approve of her conduct—rather than how dangerous the offender is."

Other critics say that notification is the wrong approach to take with sex offenders. Jerome Miller, who treats both offenders and victims at Virginia's Augustus Institute, says that whereas notifi-

> *"The constitutional rights to privacy...have not been found to preclude notification laws."*

cation leads to the isolation of sex offenders, "treatment necessitates a move toward better socialization." But can treatment help? The answer is an uncomfortable "maybe." Margaret A. Alexander, clinical director of the Wisconsin Sex Offender Treatment Program, analyzed 68 studies of treatment programs and found that treatment could reduce recidivism from 19 percent to 11 percent. But a number of states have slashed their funding for sex-offender treatment. And even for offenders who do receive treatment "you can't use the word 'cure,'" says Prentky, noting the compulsive nature of sex crimes. "For sex offenders, you can reduce the probability of reoffense. Does anyone assert all child molesters can be helped? Absolutely not."

Other criminal justice experts point to the need for stricter sentencing. Offenders who commit forcible sexual assault serve on average less than four years in prison, according to psychology professor Nathanial Pallone. "If we assiduously enforced the penalties that are on the books, that would incapacitate people for a far longer period of time," he notes. Prentky stresses the need for "intensive, possibly lifetime supervision for men who are considered to be dangerous, by supervisors with very small caseloads, who are trained to deal with sex offenders, and know what the red flags are. It will do a hell of a lot more to reduce repeat behavior than just notifying the neighbors."

Elizabeth Schroeder, the associate director of the ACLU of Southern California and the mother of two young daughters, sympathizes with both sides, but comes down against notification. "The police's job is not the public's job. Law enforcement shouldn't be a private responsibility." But a year and a half after her daughter's murder, Maureen Kanka disagrees. "It won't save all children—but it will save some. Awareness is the greatest tool that we as parents have."

"Offenders who commit forcible sexual assault serve on average less than four years in prison..."

The End of Privacy[6]

The title of this article may sound ominous, but it is intended to convey the stark reality that our personal privacy may gradually be coming to an end. Reports intimating the imminent death of privacy frequently appear in the media, while polls show that a vast majority of Americans are quite worried about escalating privacy invasions. But this pervasive concern seems to be accompanied by a fatalistic attitude among many Americans who simply accept their loss of privacy as an unfortunate consequence of the information age, a necessary cost of doing business when information is the economy's most vital commercial asset.

Still, one wonders how this could have happened. What accounts for the Government's ineptitude in safeguarding our privacy rights? Is privacy regarded by ordinary citizens and public policy makers as a trivial right unworthy of their attention? Or are we the powerless victims of technology that has stripped away our privacy without our ability to recognize what was happening?

"The concept of privacy is not easily defined."

The Importance of Privacy

Before plunging into a discussion of these questions, let me briefly review why privacy is so important. Corporate America has a penchant for implicitly downplaying the right to privacy. Arguments persist that the erosion of privacy is not such a big deal; the economic benefits of information availability and mobility, it is said, outweigh limitations on our personal privacy. Is privacy an ethical nicety, an expendable luxury, then, or is it a basic natural right that needs legal protection?

The concept of privacy is not easily defined. Perhaps the most basic and inclusive definition dates back to a seminal 1890 Harvard Law Review article written by Samuel Warren and Louis Brandeis. They differentiated the right to privacy from other legal rights and defined it as the right to be left alone, that is, the right to some measure of solitude in one's life.

It is possible to distinguish several types of privacy such as psychological privacy or communication privacy. The focus of my attention here, however, is "informational privacy." Defined simply, the right to informational privacy is the right to control the disclosure of and access to one's personal information.

Some philosophers and legal scholars have argued that privacy is an intrinsic good, implying that the right to privacy is fundamental and irreducible. Others contend that privacy is more of an instrumental good. Hence the right to privacy is derived from other rights such as property, bodily security and freedom. While

---

[6] Article by Richard A. Spinello, associate dean of faculties at Boston College, Chestnut Hill, Mass., and an adjunct assistant professor in its Carroll School of Management, from *America* 176:9-13 Ja 4-11 '97. Copyright © 1997 *America*. Reprinted with permission.

both approaches have validity, the latter seems more compelling. It is especially persuasive when applied to those rights involving our liberty and personal autonomy. A primary moral foundation for the value of privacy is its role as a condition of freedom: A shield of privacy is absolutely essential if one is freely to pursue his or her projects or cultivate intimate social relationships.

If people know that I am watching them, compiling a record of their activities or monitoring their conversations, they are apt to be more self-conscious and preoccupied with whether their statements or actions meet my approval. Besides causing such inhibitions, those who violate our private space by acquiring confidential information without permission may use it to exercise control over our activities.

Thus there is a close relationship between privacy and freedom. It is quite difficult to exercise the liberties guaranteed by the Constitution when our actions are on display or when intimate information about our lives is in the public domain. If our privacy continues to evanesce in the wake of technology's unrelenting progress, so too will our basic freedoms.

"The 1974 Privacy Act gives individuals the right to access and correct their personal records..."

Legal Protection

The present privacy laws have oblique roots in the U.S. Constitution. Various Supreme Court rulings have held that the Constitution bestows on individuals some right of privacy in accordance with the First, Fourth, Ninth and Fourteenth Amendments. Only the Fourteenth Amendment provides a basis for protecting a person's "informational privacy," since this amendment has been frequently invoked to protect citizens against certain forms of covert surveillance such as unwarranted wiretapping.

In addition, several laws enacted by Congress have been designed to protect the right to privacy. These include the Fair Credit Reporting Act of 1971, the Right to Financial Privacy Act of 1978 and the landmark 1974 Privacy Act, which deals with the protection of privacy in the use or distribution of government records. The 1974 Privacy Act gives individuals the right to access and correct their personal records and prevents information from being used for other purposes without consent. But it applies only to Federal agencies. Hence a patchwork of varied legislation exists at the state and Federal levels, but there is no comprehensive set of laws clearly delineating the extent of privacy rights.

This means that there are few regulations governing the secondary uses of information in the private sector. As a result, if companies collect information for a specific purpose (e.g., to grant credit) they can resell it or reuse it for other purposes with impunity. Where there are limitations on the secondary use of information they are usually vague and difficult to enforce. For example, the Fair Credit Reporting Act prohibits the secondary use of credit data except for "legitimate business purposes." The credit bureau industry has interpreted this criterion quite broadly. In the past they have sold credit information to data brokers for marketing purposes and still provide it to banks for prescreening credit card prospects.

This lack of comprehensive legal protection for privacy rights has opened the way for privacy's slow demise. Treating information as a commodity is a lucrative business, and financial incentives have prevailed over the recognition of privacy rights. We can appreciate the scope of this problem by examining privacy erosion in three key areas: consumer privacy, financial privacy and medical privacy.

The End of Consumer Privacy

Prior to the digital revolution consumers enjoyed almost complete privacy about their affairs. There were no computers compiling patterns of consumer spending or assembling on-line dossiers. But almost every corporation now selling to the public dutifully tracks such spending patterns. This may not seem so significant or harmful, but our purchases can be quite revealing. A subscription to the Gay Times probably reveals one's sexual orientation, while the frequent purchase of Club Med vacations may be indicative of one's lifestyle.

"...almost every corporation now selling to the public dutifully tracks such spending patterns."

The emergence of database technology in the early 1980's made it possible to store, retrieve and disseminate copious amounts of information efficiently and economically. During this period our personal data were transferred to computerized records that became the foundation of consumer profiles. These profiles were often based on public records sold by government agencies at the state and local levels. For instance, car registration and license information constitute a major source of marketing data used to reach certain groups of consumers.

Another source of data for these systems has been the information generated by various consumer transactions, such as telephone or mail orders, memberships and warranty cards, that can serve as the building blocks for richly detailed customer records. Marriott Hotels, for instance, collects the names of its hotel guests and matches them with motor vehicle and property records. It then employs special software tools to determine who is most likely to respond to their mailings. Database functionality has made it possible to profile the consumer as never before and to develop highly effective, targeted marketing campaigns.

Many individuals and organizations are now relying more heavily on digital networks as they routinely communicate by E-mail, post messages to electronic bulletin boards on the Internet and visit web sites. But in the process they become more exposed and vulnerable to those seeking to collect and sell their personal data. When users visit web sites they often fill out detailed personal profiles that become grist for marketing lists sold to third parties.

Digital networks have also made consumer information even

more widely and easily available. The use of these networks greatly expands the capability of checking up on someone's personal background or receiving an electronic list of prospective customers quickly and inexpensively. Indeed we are moving perilously close to the reality of immediate on-line personal data. Consider the recently deployed system of Yahoo, Inc., listing the names, addresses and telephone numbers of 90 million people nationwide, available at its web site with an automatic search facility. And a new database of Lexis-Nexis providing the same on-line information also included social security numbers until protests on the Internet forced their removal. Given this trend, however, it may not be long before some vendor provides a more robust on-line repository of personal data.

"...government data banks have usually provided the building blocks for these records."

The impending introduction of digital cash or electronic currency is another portent of things to come. This electronic cash might be stored on a "smart card" with a computer chip embedded in plastic. This too may seem fairly innocuous, but since one's identity will be on this card it will be possible for interested companies to track every purchase we make, not just those made with credit cards. An omniscient database will know what magazines I've purchased at the corner news-stand, which museums I frequent or what kind of over-the-counter medicine I buy. If this does happen, the residual anonymity we still enjoy as consumers may soon be irretrievably lost.

The End of Financial Privacy

More disturbing than the loss of our privacy as consumers is the loss of privacy about our financial affairs. Once again government data banks have usually provided the building blocks for these records. Certain financial information that was always in the public domain, such as real estate and bankruptcy records, is now treated as a basic commodity. Data brokers such as Information America, Inc. allow their subscribers quick on-line access to the county and court records for many states. Their vast databases contain business records, bankruptcy records, lawsuit information and property records, including liens and judgments.

By computerizing these real estate records, liens, incorporations, licenses and so on, they become more than public documents. They are now on-line commodities, more easily accessed and distributed than their physical counterparts. In addition, this data can be recombined with other on-line information to construct an in-depth profile of an individual's personal and financial background.

Some of our most sensitive financial information is included in the credit records maintained by the major credit bureaus, Equifax, TRW and TransUnion. Anyone who has taken out a car loan or mortgage or uses credit cards has a file in the computers of these bureaus. In recent years they have begun compiling records for people who do not borrow money by accessing things like utility or electric bill records. Businesses or individuals with a "legitimate business need" can order an individual's credit record. Banks, employers, insurers, landlords are some of the "legitimate" users of this service. The credit report provides a wealth of personal and financial information including an individual's social security number, the balance on one's mortgage, data about bank loans, student loans and any other credit granted over the past seven years, bill payment records (if available), credit card accounts and limits, current employer, previous addresses, data about birth and so on.

Further, because of lower computer costs the credit report itself has become a low cost commodity with little overhead. For example, major clients can purchase Equifax credit reports for one dollar. As the price drops many more industries, such as utilities and auto insurers, are relying on this report, since they find it to be a strong predictor of how well consumers will behave. But should the local electric company have access to the detailed financial records of its customers? Since the "Big Three" only make money when they distribute credit data, they have no inducement to restrict access.

The End of Medical Privacy

The most recent assault on privacy has developed in the health care industry, in which patient records have also become commodities for sale. These records, containing highly sensitive and revealing information, are being collected and stored in databases maintained by hospitals, H.M.O.'s, pharmaceutical companies and data brokers specializing in medical information. Furthermore, as genetic information becomes more readily available, medical records will not only reveal one's present medical condition but also one's future health prospects.

A growing number of third-party companies handle such medical information—IMS America, for instance, or PCN (Physicians Computer Network). They specialize in gathering information on patient illnesses and the drugs prescribed for those illnesses. IMS has admitted that patient names are often included when they purchase this data from H.M.O.'s or drug store chains. This company is careful enough to remove those names along with other identifiers, but will other organizations be as conscientious?

Obviously the practice itself raises many questions. Is it morally acceptable for physicians and pharmacists to entrust such sensitive information to these brokers without the knowledge and consent of their patients? Is such a practice truly consistent with the obligations of information stewardship? And shouldn't there be stricter safeguards to ensure that personal identifiers (name, social security number) are never included with this data?

The Medical Information Bureau is another organization that functions as a broker of medical records. Whenever someone applies for life or health insurance, a background check is initiated in order to verify the accuracy of the medical data and his-

"...as genetic information becomes more readily available, medical records will not only reveal one's present medical condition but also one's future health prospects."

tory reported by the applicant. The insurance company will first check the M.I.B., and it will also turn over to the M.I.B. the results of its findings. The expanding M.I.B. database already includes over 15 million records.

Presently the M.I.B. does restrict access to these files to its member insurance companies. They are not made available to any third parties such as employers or government agencies. There are, however, no restrictions on how insurance companies or their investigators use this data, so it could conceivably enter the public domain through these sources. Some insurance companies, for example, do provide detailed medical data to employers.

Hospitals are also culprits in contributing to the porosity of the medical community. Some hospitals hold "free" health clinics to screen for high blood pressure or other potential problems, but the results end up in a database used for future marketing campaigns. In most Boston area hospitals a patient's entire medical record is entered on-line without a patient's knowledge. Doctors and other authorized users at affiliated hospitals can access these records, which sometimes include psychiatric data.

"Congress has been considering a significant piece of legislation, the Bennett-Leahy bill, that would make it illegal to sell medical data to marketers."

Currently, no Federal laws protect the confidentiality of medical records. Congress has been considering a significant piece of legislation, the Bennett-Leahy bill, that would make it illegal to sell medical data to marketers. It would also guarantee individuals an opportunity to see and correct their medical records. This well-intentioned effort, however, has met with strident opposition, since critics claim it would actually expedite the development of health care databases. Access to these databases would be given to "health information trustees," a broad category including medical researchers, the insurance industry, law enforcement agencies and so forth. Critics claim that this legislation would promote the dissemination of medical data rather than protect patient privacy.

Thus, medical privacy seems destined to be another victim of our evolving information technologies. By putting so much medical data on-line without proper safeguards the government, the health care industry and the information industry are clearly undermining the foundation of the confidential doctor-patient relationship.

The Cumulative Effect

It seems quite evident that our right to informational privacy has been sacrificed for the sake of economic efficiency and other social objectives. As our personal information becomes tangled in the web of information technology, our control over how that data will be utilized and distributed is notably diminished. Our personal background and purchases are tracked by many companies that consider us prospects for their products or services; our financial profile and credit history is available to a plethora of "legitimate" users, and our medical records are more widely accessible than ever before. The net effect is that each of us can become an open book to anyone who wants to take the time to investigate our background.

Another adverse consequence of all this is that we can be more easily targeted and singled out either as individuals or as members of certain groups. Database technology makes it easy to find and exploit certain groups based on age, income level, place of residence or purchasing habits. At the same time on-line data banks now make it especially simple to pinpoint individuals electronically.

Also, the construction of consumer or financial profiles often means that we are being stereotyped on the basis of certain characteristics. This may result in prejudicial or unfair treatment by those with access to those profiles. As the information in these profiles becomes more sensitive, the greater is the likelihood of detrimental effects from this prejudice. It is one thing to be stereotyped as a candidate for luxury vacations, but quite another to be classified as a health risk or segregated for one's apparent political views. We must not fail to recognize that the collection of personal data empowers organizations to use that information as a means of controlling our access to the goods and services that are necessary for a decent life in our society.

"...on-line data banks now make it especially simple to pinpoint individuals electronically."

A Prescription for Privacy

If public policy makers do become convinced that privacy is worth preserving, what should be done? Are there any viable solutions? Further complicating the issue, of course, are legitimate economic considerations. Privacy cannot be accomplished without incurring some costs. And we cannot ignore the economic benefits of acquiring and distributing information and using data as a commercial tool to target the right customers. If the information flow about consumers is overly constrained, a substantial negative economic impact cannot be discounted.

Given this need for balance between privacy rights and requirements for precise information, the most viable solution seems to be some form of informed consent, which would require the information collector to gain permission for subsequent reuse of data. The model of informed consent can be implemented in one of two ways: 1) the "opt-in" approach, which requires individuals to give explicit approval for secondary uses of their personal information; 2) the "opt-out" approach, whereby individuals are notified that their personal data will be used for secondary purposes unless they disapprove and notify the vendor within a certain time frame. If informed consent is to work properly consumers must have knowledge and opportunity. They must be made aware of any projected reuse in a timely fashion and be given a reasonable opportunity to restrict it.

The adoption of the less stringent "opt-out" approach does achieve some balance between economic efficiency and privacy rights. Organizations would still have access to vast amounts of consumer information, though the cost of acquiring that information would be marginally higher. And consumers would have more of an opportunity to protect their privacy and to control how their personal information is shared with others.

In addition, there must be stricter controls for especially sensitive information such as medical data. The Bennett-Leahy bill is a good start but it seems evident that even tighter controls on commercial applications involving health care data are essential. Also, if a centralized national database becomes a reality, it will be necessary to achieve a broad public consensus on the definition of the health care trustees who should have access to that data.

In summary, then, if informed consent is made mandatory for the reuse of consumer data and there are stricter safeguards for more critical information such as medical data, we can begin to make some progress in protecting privacy rights. But unless we soon come to terms with this problem the boundaries between what is public and private could become much more tenuous. A world where privacy is in such short supply will undermine our freedom and dignity and pose a grave threat to our security and well-being.

II. Privacy and the Workplace

Editor's Introduction

The issue of privacy rights in the workplace, a subject of particular concern at the present moment, is the focus of Section Two. In the opening article, Mark Frankel in *The New Republic* notes that because of concern with worker productivity, industrial espionage, personal security, drugs on the job, and skyrocketing insurance liability, corporate America is increasingly resorting to secretly monitoring its employees. Managers not only listen in on employees' phone calls but also search their computer files, voice mail messages, and E-mail. Although many people believe that because they have private passwords only they can enter their E-mail, the fact is those who monitor employees can override passwords easily. Privacy advocates and labor unions have attempted to promote legislation restricting workplace surveillance, but they have been opposed by such groups as the National Association of Manufacturers, and no new legislation has resulted. In a related article, Thomas Clavin, in the *Ladies' Home Journal*, announces that about forty million employees are being secretly monitored at work. Moreover, everything an employee does on a computer can easily be called up by the boss; even erased files can continue to exist for some time. Hidden video cameras (some smaller than a thimble) and microphones can be concealed. Employee suits for invasion of privacy, however, have rarely proved successful because employers have vital interests of their own to protect, and the courts have generally favored them.

The ACLU's special report (effective September 1996) on surveillance in the workplace gives an up-to-date and informed look at present conditions. They find that the number of people subjected to electronic surveillance in the workplace has increased markedly in the last six years. In addition, the percentage of major companies requiring urine drug testing has climbed from 38% to 70%. New threats to privacy include genetic testing and "active badges"— clip-on microcomputers that allow employers to track a worker's movements electronically. Telephone calls also continue to be monitored; one source estimates that employers eavesdrop on an estimated 400 million telephone calls every year. Over 70% of major U. S. firms tested employees for drugs in 1996—a figure that includes both routine testing and random testing of employees, whether or not they have ever exhibited any drug-related problems. According to the report, genetic testing also poses a particularly serious threat to privacy, since it can lead to "genetic discrimination": the refusal to hire or the termination of employees who are at risk of developing genetic disorders.

The following article by Peter Cassidy in *The Progressive* deals with a proposal by the U. S. Commission on Immigration Reform for a federally-mandated I.D. card designed to discourage the hiring of illegal immigrants. Although the government chose not to act on the commission's recommendation, it remains a possibility for the future and poses the threat of excessive government control over citizen's lives. The concluding article, by Michael Losey in *USA Today*, deals with increasing interventions in employees' private lives. It is wondered if these interventions will come to include an employee's life outside of the job. Will that employee be prohibited from smoking at home, as well as at the office? Some companies already prohibit off-site consumption of alcohol. Losey predicts that in the next few years a stronger effort will be made to enact or expand workplace privacy laws.

Candid Camera[1]

I used to think professional snoops were all variations on Harry
Caul, the paranoid, guilt-ridden wiretapper of Francis Ford
Coppola's *The Conversation*. But W.T. "Ted" Sandin clearly loves
his work. With the infectious enthusiasm of a high-school camera club faculty adviser, the middle-aged Sandin runs Video
Systems Inc., one of the country's leading manufacturers and dis-
tributors of covert video surveillance hardware. At Surveillance
Expo '95, which brought several hundred private investigators
and corporate security specialists (plus a smattering of Armani-
clad Middle Eastern and Latin American gentlemen too discreet
to expose their affiliations) to the McLean Hilton in Virginia last
summer, Sandin was among the top draws. About three dozen
conferees paid $100 each to attend his seminar on how to spy on
other people in the electronic age.

He did not disappoint. Reminding his scribbling pupils that
"surveillance means only extension of the eye," Sandin spent
four hours demonstrating a collection of eye-popping miniature
video cameras, each seemingly tinier than the last. The smallest
was a black-and-white TV camera barely larger than a piece of
Bazooka bubble gum. Attached to a tiny transmitter powered by
a common 9-volt battery, such minicams can be hidden almost
anywhere in a typical office or factory, Sandin explained. Light
switches, exit signs or room thermostats are just a few of the possibilities for camouflage. "Be creative," he exhorted us.

In the name of personal security, Americans have already
learned to accept and ignore video cameras in the public spaces
they routinely pass through: parking lots, elevators, bank lobbies
and hotel stair-ways. (According to STAT Resources, a
Massachusetts research firm, an estimated $2.1 billion will be
spent on closed-circuit video gear this year alone.) Now they
may have to learn to accept them in the workplace as well.
Propelled by concerns with worker productivity, industrial espionage, personal security, drugs on the job and skyrocketing
insurance liability, corporate America is increasingly resorting to
secret monitoring of its employees. An August 1994 report by the
Geneva-based International Labor Organization concluded that
"Monitoring and surveillance techniques available as a result of
advances in technology make methods of control more pervasive
than ever before and raise serious questions of human rights."

Consider a few recent cases. In Phoenix, Arizona, Freddy
Graig, a longtime elementary school principal, stumbled upon a
video camera hidden in the ceiling of his suburban school
office—as well as one secreted in the school shower he often

"...minicams can be hidden almost anywhere in a typical office or factory..."

1 Article by Mark Frankel, author, from *The New Republic* 214:11-12 My 20, '96.
Copyright © 1996 *The New Republic*. Reprinted with permission.

used after jogging. The cameras had been installed by the newly hired school district superintendent, who claimed that Craig was under investigation for unspecified "misconduct" with his students' parents. The charges proved groundless.

In Elmira, New York, a former McDonald's restaurant manager went to court seeking $2 million from the burger chain, as well as the local franchise, for invasion of privacy. In addition to overseeing the deep fryer and griddle, the plaintiff, Michael Huffcut, had been conducting an extramarital affair with another McDonald's employee. Huffcut's suit charged that not only did his former restaurant supervisor obtain copies of the romantic messages the illicit lovers left for each other on their office voice mail, he also played the recordings for Huffcut's wife.

Several years ago, the Boston Sheraton Hotel installed a hidden camera in the employees' locker room in what management claimed was an effort to crack a drug ring—and what lawyers for the hotel workers describe as a heavy-handed attempt to discourage union activity.

The threat is not limited to videocams and voice mail. Service industries place millions of workers in front of computer terminals where their performance is easily monitored by remote. Desktop computers, fax machines, pagers, computer networks, cellular phones and e-mail have become as ubiquitous as styrofoam coffee cups in most offices. While employees have been introduced to these contraptions with soothing talk about "personal passwords" and "private files," workers' privacy is easily shredded. In one of the few surveys of corporate electronic privacy policies, conducted by *MacWorld* magazine in 1993, of 301 U.S. companies polled, more than one in five had searched their employees' computer files, voice mail, e-mail or other digital network communications. "Users naturally assume that, because they have private passwords, only they can enter their e-mail and private files,...but even the most insignificant network managers can override passwords and enter files," says Charles Pillar, who conducted the survey.

While researching this article, I struck up an e-mail correspondence with a New York-based high-tech surveillance specialist who told me about his work:

"For a cellular phone interception system, I charge $2,500 to $4,000. This allows the employer to monitor all employees' cellular phone conversations or simply to keep a log of the times and length of calls and any numbers called, etc. It is not actually necessary to listen in on the conversations; they can be logged into a computer. The employer can thus see who has been using these phones for personal use to make $2-a-minute personal calls to the kids....

I've been called to do phone interception work a lot, especially with telemarketer and service representative type workers where the boss monitors the line to make sure that the employees don't have a nasty tone with the customers....

For computer modem interception, I usually charge $3,000. It allows an employer to passively monitor a particular telephone line and intercept the modem data that's going through [it]. The employer can, in effect, see everything that the employee types into his computer and that appears on his screen."

Most American workers assume that their privacy on the job is ensured by constitutional safeguards. Unfortunately, they are wrong. While the Fourth Amendment protects citizens against unreasonable search and seizure by the state, it does not touch private employers, who are free to run their businesses—and spy on their employees—as they please. Current federal privacy laws are case studies in half-measures. While the 1986 Electronic Communications Act prohibits eavesdropping on telephones without a warrant or permission, it provides a loophole that permits companies to monitor employees' calls "for business purposes." And, while privacy laws vary widely from state to state, cutting-edge gizmos such as mini-video cameras are so new they slip between existing wiretap statutes and labor regulations.

Privacy advocates, labor unions and groups such as 9 to 5, the working women's lobby, have long sought national standards that would regulate workplace surveillance. In the last Congress, Senator Paul Simon and Representative Pat Williams introduced such legislation, the Privacy for Consumers and Workers Act. But the U.S. Chamber of Commerce and the National Association of Manufacturers (NAM) opposed the bill fiercely, and it died in committee. Privacy advocates have all but given up on trying to pass a meaningful piece of legislation this session.

Until Congress puts on the brakes, video cameras and other means of workplace surveillance will only get cooler, and more insidious. Back at the Surveillance Expo, Ted Sandin proudly demonstrated the latest thing: body video. Wearing a tiny camera hidden in a pair of plastic sunglasses, he strutted about the stage. In the audience, we watched, mesmerized, as an image of ourselves jiggled on a nearby video monitor. Sandin promised that as marvelous as this micro-gadgetry seemed, even niftier stuff was coming down the pike. After all, he reminded us, "this is a consumer-driven marketplace."

"...while privacy laws vary widely from state to state, cutting-edge gizmos such as mini-video cameras are so new they slip between existing wiretap statutes and labor regulations."

Is Your Boss Spying on You?[2]

Rhonda Hall and Bonita Bourke worked for the Nissan Motor Corporation in Southern California as employee trainers at various dealerships. To coordinate their efforts they kept in touch via E-mail, a system of sending messages from one employee's computer to another. Their messages occasionally contained disparaging remarks about upper management. What Hall and Bourke didn't know was that their messages were being read by management—until their boss called them in and reprimanded them. The women complained to higher-ups in the company that their privacy had been violated.

They sued for invasion of privacy. Nissan argued that as owner of the computer system it had the right to object to the way employees used their computers. In a pretrial proceeding, the court ruled in favor of the company.

Though it may seem like something out of the movie *Disclosure*, such electronic spying in the workplace has become more and more widespread. As companies take advantage of increasingly sophisticated technology, employees are finding that their actions, conversations and even personal lives are under scrutiny by their bosses. What's more, most of this spying is perfectly legal. The only relevant existing federal law is one that forbids employers' knowingly listening in on workers' personal phone calls. "The potential is there in the workplace to find out almost anything about you," says Joseph Weintraub, Ph.D., a management professor at Babson College, in Wellesley, Massachusetts, and a corporate consultant.

Of course, it's always been true that an unscrupulous boss could sneak into a worker's office after hours and read her telephone messages or go through her files. But today's high-tech advances allow management to pry much more easily. Anyone who works on a video-display terminal, electronic telephone console or other computer-based equipment, such as laser-scanner cash registers, which record for management how many items a cashier scans per minute, may be under surveillance. "Workers are becoming more vulnerable as the technology expands," says Milind Shah, spokesperson for the American Civil Liberty Union's (ACLU) National Task Force on Civil Liberties in the Workplace, in New York City. "And they are being judged—and sometimes even fired—based less on performance than on what employers see or hear them do."

Although no organization keeps precise figures on how many employees across the U.S. are subject to such company surveillance, Jeffery Miller, spokesperson for the Washington, D.C.-

"The only relevant existing federal law is one that forbids employers' knowingly listening in on workers' personal phone calls."

---

[2] Article by Thomas Clavin, a journalist, from *Ladies' Home Journal*® 112:76-83. Ap '95. Copyright © 1995 Meredith Corporation. All rights reserved. Reprinted with permission.

based Communications Workers of America, believes that the number is in the tens of millions. "Based on feedback from our members, studies I've seen and the proliferation of sophisticated systems...I believe the figure is close to forty million workers," he says.

Just how do companies spy on their employees? A few common methods are:

Computer monitoring. Everything a worker does on her computer is easily accessible to her boss. He can simply call up her files and read them anytime. What many employees don't know is that deleting a file doesn't mean that it's irretrievable. Erased files can continue to exist for some time in cyberspace.

Yet even more insidious is using computers to track a worker's activities. "I have to log off the computer when I go to the bathroom, and log back on when I return," says Cathy Greer,* thirty-three, who works for an answering service in Pennsylvania. "I have the feeling the whole system is watching me—where I go, how long I take, even what I do."

Telephone taps. Although federal law does prohibit employers from listening in on personal phone calls, bosses are within their rights when monitoring employees' business-related calls. This is especially pervasive in companies that depend heavily on customer service, such as catalog sales and insurance firms. But it also means that workers who make personal calls from the office—and let's face it, who doesn't?—may have an unethical boss listening in.

Jean Engel-Madura is an airline reservation agent in New York who doesn't mind that her supervisors occasionally listen in on calls from prospective travelers. "What I didn't know was that the phone system was also geared toward recording conversations among the reservationists," she says. "One day I was called in by my supervisor, who brought up personal comments I'd made to others in the office. It was scary, like anything you say can be used against you."

Voice-mail violations. Voice mail is usually part of a company-wide system, so all a boss has to do is go into an employee's office when she's not there and play her messages. Even if the voice-mail system requires a password to access messages, a curious boss may be able to get that information from the employee's personnel records, where it's usually listed for sensible business reasons—if, for example, the employee is out sick and a colleague has to cover for her.

E-mail espionage. E-mail offers easy, fast communication, but it can also be easily intercepted by a boss.

*Name has been changed.

> *"What many employees don't know is that deleting a file doesn't mean that it's irretrievable."*

Any employee who sends a message to a co-worker complaining about her job, or confiding personal information about, say, her marriage, could be "caught" by her supervisor.

Hidden video cameras and microphones. A camera and microphone can be installed in workers' offices or in employee lounges and cafeterias to record what she's doing and talking about, as well as how much time she spends socializing. There have even been a few reported instances of hidden cameras installed in company rest rooms. Today, says the ACLU's Milind Shah, "a camera can be no larger than a thimble, and a microphone may be even smaller."

"There have even been a few reported instances of hidden cameras installed in company rest rooms."

Secret tracking systems. Some employers use sophisticated electronic devices to keep tabs on their workers' comings and goings—and the employees never know it. Take the case of Alice Kolb,* thirty, an executive at a toy-manufacturing company in Connecticut, who spent her lunch hours visiting her infant daughter at her baby-sitter's house nearby. One day the company president sent Alice a printout that showed the times she'd left and returned to work for the past several weeks; it indicated that on many days she'd been late getting back to the office. Alice was stunned. Unknown to her or any of the other employees, the office security system—which required each worker to insert a plastic card into a machine upon entering or leaving—also served as a time clock.

Such stories are becoming commonplace. "Just as years ago there were sweatshops, there are workplaces now that are electronic sweatshops," says Alan F. Westin, Ph.D., a professor of political science at Columbia University, in New York City, and the publisher of *Privacy & American Business*, a bimonthly newsletter. "This issue will increase in importance during the next few years as we try to figure out what workplace technology should or should not do and how much privacy workers can reasonably expect."

The Right to Spy?

Until more laws are in place, however, employers can continue to monitor workers with relatively few restrictions. "Many workers have a reasonable expectation of privacy, but you shouldn't expect the same protection" at work that you have at home, says Jeffrey Kingston, a lawyer in San Francisco who's an expert in computer law. When an employee sues a company for invasion of privacy, "for the most part, the courts have gone along with the employer."

Part of the problem is that lawmakers simply haven't kept pace with technological advances. The Privacy for Consumers and Workers Act, sponsored by Senator Paul Simon (D-Illinois),

*Name has been changed.

would require employers in all companies to inform new workers that they'll be monitored and to describe the type of monitoring, its frequency and how the collected data will be used. The bill was introduced in Congress last year—for the second time. No decision has been made on whether it will be reintroduced this year.

Most business groups oppose the bill. Dan Yager, general counsel for the Labor Policy Association, in Washington, D.C., a lobbying group that represents business interests, contends that privacy laws on the books in many states are sufficient. "More legislation is not necessary," he says.

For employers, monitoring workers is simply good business. It's one way they can protect their company's interests and prevent employees from taking advantage of them. "There are cases of employees using the facilities and equipment to engage in illegal acts, like gambling," Yager says.

"Others claim they monitor employees as a way to ensure their safety."

Many managers also worry that disgruntled or dishonest workers might be passing along confidential business information to competitors or sabotaging company operations. Others claim they monitor employees as a way to ensure their safety. "To some extent, legitimate monitoring offers an opportunity to detect people whose workplace behavior indicates a serious problem," says Yager.

Finally, for many employers the bottom line is that it's their company, and they have a right to make sure that workers are doing their job. "It outrages me that some self-appointed privacy advocates say that all monitoring violates consumer rights, " says business and privacy expert Alan Westin. "Electronic monitoring is appropriate when it is done to [protect] work that affects the success or failure of the business and when fair monitoring practices are followed."

Paying the Price

But many employees say that rather than increasing productivity, office surveillance makes it harder to do their jobs. "It exacerbates the stress level that already exists on the job," says Cindia Cameron, national program and organizing director in the Atlanta office of 9 to 5, National Association of Working Women. "If every time you make a call or send a message someone is listening or watching, you never get a break."

Besides adding to office tension, employee monitoring can also chip away at a worker's loyalty and dedication to her company. Says Joseph Weintraub, "It can't help when a company that's asking for trust and loyalty is snooping on workers."

Employees agree. "It's already stressful for me to be working six or seven hours without a break, but it's worse to know everything I do or say is being monitored," says Cathy Greer, the answering-service operator in Pennsylvania. "The constant surveillance gets to you."

How to Protect Yourself

What should an employee do if she is being monitored at work, or fears she might be? Experts say there are several steps workers can take:

Urge your company to create an official policy on workplace monitoring. This can be done through a union or an ad hoc committee, and it need not be confrontational. If both management and employees are flexible, you can develop a system everyone can live with. "Employers should...specify the goals of monitoring, like connecting it to production," Weintraub says. Once you've agreed upon a policy, have it written up and distributed to every employee.

"If both management and employees are flexible, you can develop a system everyone can live with."

Take precautions. If you become aware that your company is monitoring you, raise objections to snooping. One big risk: Your boss could accuse you—or even fire you—for insubordination. The best strategy, therefore, is prevention: Change your E-mail or computer terminal password every month (or even every week) to make it more difficult for someone to gain access, and be creative about it—never use an obvious code such as your name or your child's name. Always store or delete data, thus removing it from your computer monitor, whenever you leave your desk.

Finally, be careful about what you do in the workplace. "You wouldn't publish a nasty letter about your boss in the company newsletter or leave a personal memo around the office. Email or a computer file is not a license to be privately negative," says Alan Westin. "Use the same discretion you would use in any form of communication, and think twice about revealing intimate information."

Get help if you think your workplace rights have been violated. For advice or assistance contact: The Job Survival Hotline operated by 9 to 5, National Association of Working Women. Call toll-free at 800-522-0925 between the hours of 10 A.M. and 4 P.M., E.T. The American Bar Association. Write ABA Publications, P.O. Box 10892, Chicago, IL 60610-0892, or call 312-988-5522, and ask for the booklet "Law in the Workplace" (the cost is $2.50, plus S2.00 for handling). The ACLU's National Task Force on Civil Liberties in the Workplace. Call 212-944-9800, extension 416, for more information on this issue.

Surveillance, Incorporated[3]

American Workers Forfeit Privacy for a Paycheck
An ACLU Special Report
Sept. 1996

Introduction

In December 1990, the American Civil Liberties Union announced the formation of its National Task Force on Civil Liberties in the Workplace with the publication of a special report, *A State of Emergency in the American Workplace.* The report, authored by Task Force Coordinator Lewis L. Maltby, described the dearth of legal protections for private sector employees in the areas of free speech, due process, equality and privacy, and recommended remedial legislation at both the state and federal levels.

Six years later, the Task Force issues this update to its original report, with a special focus on the right to privacy. Although the ACLU and other employee rights and privacy organizations have worked hard to generate support in state legislatures for much needed legal protections in this area, these efforts have met with only moderate success. As the chart appended to this report demonstrates, state legislators have been resistant to considering, much less passing, new laws that would protect private sector workers from practices that, if carried out by the government against its citizens, would be blatantly illegal.

In the absence of legislative reform, personal privacy in the workplace is now more ephemeral than ever. We seem to be approaching a once unthinkable "brave new world" in which a worker's every move can be monitored with total legal impunity. In heavily computerized industries today, for example, workers are monitored not only by time clocks, but also by their computer terminals and their telephone keypads. Too many trips to the bathroom can be grounds for discipline. Being "unplugged" from their "job monitors" without permission can lead to dismissal.

Since our last report six years ago
—The number of people subject to electronic surveillance at work has increased from approximately 8 million to more than 20 million.
—The percentage of major companies subjecting their current employees to urine drug testing has climbed from 38% to 70%.
—Major new threats to employee privacy, such as genetic testing

---

[3] Article by staffwriter, from ACLU Special Report 1-5 S '96. Courtesy of the American Civil Liberties Union. Reprinted with permission.

and "active badges"—clip-on microcomputers that allow an employer to track a workers movements electronically—have emerged.

Many of these practices cannot be justified on economic or business grounds, and some are so unfair and intrusive that we must question whether they can be tolerated in a democratic society.

Electronic Monitoring

Electronic monitoring in the workplace can and does take many different forms, and surveillance technology is definitely a growth industry. One form of electronic monitoring, done by computer, may include searches of employee computer files, voicemail, email and other networking communications. In 1987, the Congressional Office of Technology Assessment estimated that six to eight million people were subjected to electronic surveillance at work. When in 1993, the computer magazine *Macworld* conducted a nationwide survey of 301 businesses of all sizes in a wide range of industries, almost 22 percent said they engaged in electronic monitoring-mostly without the knowledge or consent of their employees. The survey found that less than one-third of the companies gave their employees advance warning of their monitoring practices, and only 18 percent had memorialized their practices in written policy.

Since the average company in the *Macworld* survey employed 3,240 people, the researchers concluded that "some 20 million Americans may be subject to electronic monitoring through their computers (not including telephones) on the job." Assuming this growth trend has continued since 1993, today 40 million employees, or one out of every three in the American workforce, are electronically surveyed by their employers. Three years later, that figure is sure to have climbed substantially.

Telephone monitoring affects vast numbers of employees and consumers. According to the Communications Workers of America, employers eavesdrop on an estimated 400 million telephone calls every year, or more than 750 calls every minute. Although federal law prohibits warrantless wiretapping unless one of the parties to the conversation consents, the Electronic Communication Privacy Act of 1986 exempts employer eavesdropping on job-related employee telephone conversations. This amounts to a carte blanche to listen to any and all conversations, since an employer can legitimately argue that it can take several minutes to determine whether a conversation is personal or job-related.

Other forms of electronic monitoring include
—Headphone and audio monitoring of conversations
—Tracking devices
—Closed circuit television monitoring
—Video surveillance

> *"The survey found that less than one-third of the companies gave their employees advance warning of their monitoring practices..."*

In 1993, The Privacy for Consumers and Workers Act was introduced in Congress. Although it garnered substantial legislative
support, it still had not been enacted by the time of the 1994
election, after which all efforts to pass federal legislation in this
area were abandoned. Under the Act, which the ACLU enthusi-
astically supported, employers would be required to inform new
hires of any monitoring practices, including telephone monitoring, and give advance warning—e.g., a signal or a beep—whenever monitoring was taking place.[i] The Act also capped the total
time an employee could be monitored at two hours per week,
and prohibited secret, periodic, or random monitoring of long-
term employees.

No state has enacted protective legislation in this area, with the
partial exception of Connecticut, which does not allow monitoring "in areas designated for the health or personal comfort of
employees or for safeguarding their possessions or contract nego-
tiations."

Drug Testing

In many industries today, taking a drug test has become as routine as filling out a job application. The American Management
Association has conducted an annual survey of workplace drug
testing policies since 1987.[ii] According to the AMA's 1996 summary of key findings, "The share of major U.S. firms that test for
drugs rose to 81 percent in January 1996 from 78 percent in
January 1995, bringing workplace testing to its highest level
since AMA's initial survey in 1987."

While much of this testing is "for cause," including reasonable
suspicion of drug use and testing after accidents, a growing number of firms have instituted "periodic" or "random" testing practices, in which employees who are not suspected of drug use—
and who, in fact, are not exhibiting *any* work-related problems—
are required to take drug tests.[iii] In 1990, the year of the ACLU's
first report, periodic or random testing was carried out by 10.3
percent of large companies. Today that figure stands at 33.7 percent. Between 1987 and 1996, periodic or random drug testing in
private industry increased by 1248 percent!

Even getting a foot in the door is conditioned upon submitting
to urinalysis. Many more job applicants than current employees
are tested. Sixty-seven percent of the AMA's sample firms now
test all new hires; in 1990, that figure was 33.6 percent.
According to the AMA, the data suggests that "approximately
one-third of all U.S. new hires will undergo a drug test."

Urinalysis is still the preferred testing method, used by 92 percent of large companies. Especially when it is not for cause, urine
testing raises grave privacy concerns. First, in order to avoid
"false positive" results, the employee must reveal to the employer the names of all prescription and non-prescription drugs he or
she is taking.[iv] Second, the specimen collection process often
involves direct or indirect observation to assure the authenticity

"Between 1987 and 1996, periodic or random drug testing in private industry increased by 1248 percent!"

of the urine sample. Direct observation is an obvious invasion of personal privacy, but even indirect observation con be degrading. Typically, employees must remove all outer garments, and urinate in a bathroom in which the water supply has been turned off and blueing agent has been added to the toilet. A monitor may be posted nearby to "listen for normal sounds of urination." Third, another search takes place in the laboratory, when the urine sample is subjected to chemical scrutiny.

Although those companies that drug test their employees believe it to be an effective workplace policy, justifiable on economic and business grounds, there is scant evidence to support that belief. The AMA, as part of its 1996 survey, asked the responding companies to indicate whether or not they had gathered statistical evidence that their testing programs resulted in lesser absenteeism or illness, fewer disability claims, lower accident rates, and fewer incidents of theft and violence. Eighty percent of the companies answered in the negative—they had no such evidence. The AMA's findings are consistent with those of the National Academy of Sciences, which, in a 1994 report, concluded that "there is as yet no conclusive scientific evidence from properly controlled studies that employment drug testing programs widely discourage drug use or encourage rehabilitation."

"...workers in some states have some protection against some drug testing practices."

The ACLU and a number of labor unions have fought against unfair drug testing policies and practices in state and federal courts, in state legislatures and in Congress, but the great majority of private sector employees still have no legal protection in this area. As the appended chart shows, workers in some states have some protection against some drug testing practices. And even in those states, such laws have been attacked since their passage and have, in some cases, been significantly weakened. But for most, a refusal to submit to a drug test is grounds for discipline or termination with no legal recourse or, in the case of an applicant, a lost job opportunity.

Genetic Testing

The federal government's ambitious Human Genome Project, whose goal is to map the entire human genetic system, is well underway and will continue until at least the year 2005. Detailed knowledge of the human genetic structure will, of course, represent an enormous medical advance and will allow for early diagnosis and possibly treatment for a wide range of genetic conditions and diseases. But it also has its dangers. Although it is just in its infancy, genetic testing in the workplace poses a serious threat to personal privacy and may well lead to "genetic discrimination," i.e., the refusal to hire or the termination of employees who are at risk for developing genetic conditions, even if their condition is "latent," meaning they are completely asymptomatic at the time.

This year, several researchers published a report of a survey of at-risk individuals for reports of genetic discrimination in the workplace and several other contexts (insurance coverage, education, adoption).[v] Based on almost 1,000 returned questionnaires, almost half of which indicated that the respondent had experienced discrimination, the authors concluded, "Genetic discrimination is variable in form and cause and can have marked consequences for individuals experiencing discrimination and their relatives. The presence of abnormal genes in all individuals makes each person a potential victim of this type of discrimination. The increasing development and utilization of genetic tests will likely result in increased genetic discrimination in the absence of controvening measures."

At this point, there is no accurate count of how many companies are presently engaging in genetic testing, but it does not appear that the practice is widespread. The main disincentive, however, may be cost, and the price is coming down. One genetic test that cost $2,000 in 1991 now costs less than $800. If the cost continues to decrease, it is likely that the incidence of testing will increase. Companies can also avoid the high cost of testing by simply requiring prospective employees who have undergone genetic testing on their own initiative to release their medical records as a condition of employment.

Employers have a strong incentive to subject employees and job applicants to genetic testing. Between 85 and 90 percent of all individuals with health insurance in the U.S. are covered under employer group health plans, and employers are under enormous economic pressure to keep their health care costs down. Employing people who are at risk for serious genetic conditions, even if they are completely asymptomatic and may in fact never develop the disease, may present the employer with an unacceptable financial burden.

Only six states have enacted laws prohibiting employers from requiring employees or job applicants to undergo genetic testing (see appended chart) and none of them give adequate legal protection. At the federal level, the Americans With Disabilities Act may protect genetically tested employees from employment discrimination, but the Act has not yet been interpreted by any court to cover victims of discrimination based on latent genetic conditions. And there is no federal law that limits the right of an employer to require genetic testing.

"Employing people who are at risk for serious genetic conditions...may present the employer with an unacceptable financial burden."

Conclusion

The pervasiveness and level of surveillance being practiced today in the workplace is unprecedented in American history. Increasingly, American workers are being treated like pieces of equipment. Employers are asserting an interest so broad that it would encompass controls over what employees do and say on their breaks, off the job, or on the weekends. Like some science fiction scenario, people with the "wrong" genetic makeup would be rendered unemployable. Once an employer's insurance costs, medical bills and productivity are allowed to trump the rights of workers without any limit, then anything is possible.

The solution is clear. Now, more than ever, we need new state and federal legislation to protect all Americans' right to privacy at work.

Notes

i The Privacy for Consumers and Workers Act defines "electronic monitoring" to include "use of a computer, telephone, wire, radio, camera, identifier, accessor, locator, or other electromagnetic, photoelectronic, or photo-optical system."

ii The AMA surveys a representative sample of its corporate membership of 9,500 U.S. companies, which in total employ one-fourth of the American workforce. The 1996 sample has a 3.5% margin of error.

iii As the AMA report points out, two-thirds of these firms are testing under government mandate. The largest number are transportation companies following the Department of Transportation's drug testing requirements.

iv Certain legal compounds "cross-react" with the most common drug screens to produce a "false positive", e.g., people who take Depronil, a drug prescribed for Parkinson's Disease, will test positive for amphetamines.

v Huntington's Disease, hemochronmatosis, mucopolyssacharidoses, and phenylketonuria are among the diseases that can now be detected through testing—and, as the Human Genome Project progresses, the list is growing longer.

Appendix: Workplace Privacy Rights, State By State

State	Electronic Monitoring	Genetic Testing	Urine Testing
Alabama	None	None	None
Alaska	None	None	None
Arizona	None	None	Limited law. (Probable cause is needed to test school bus drivers. Bus driver applicants must be tested. All other employees may be randomally tested.)
Arkansas	None	None	None
California	None	None	None
Colorado	None	None	None
Connecticut	Not allowed in "areas designated for the health or personal comfort of employees or for safeguarding their possession or contract negotiations."	None	Good law. (Reasonable suspicion is required except where random testing is authorized by federal law or the employee's position is designated as high-risk or safety-sensitive or is part of an employee assistance program.)
Delware	None	None	Limited law. (Schoolbus driver applicants must be tested.)
D.C.	None	None	None
Florida	None	None	None for private employees. Good law for public employees. (Reasonable suspicion is necessary to test public employees or they may be tested for routine fitness for duty. Applicants for safety sensitive positions may be tested.)
Georgia	None	None	Limited law. (School bus drivers are subject to random testing. State employees in high-risk jobs, or applicants for such jobs, are subject to random testing.)
Hawaii	None	None	Limited law. (Procedural requirement only.)
Idaho	None	None	None
Illinois	None	None	Limited law. (Transit employees are subject to random testing.)
Indiana	None	None	None
Iowa	None	Genetic law	Good law. (Probable cause required for all testing.)
Kansas	None	None	Limited law for private employees. Limited law or good law for public employees. (Reasonable suspicion is needed to test office holders and employees with safety-sensitive government positions and employees of mental health institutions. Mandatory testing of job applicants is permissible if done to determine whether an applicant is physically capable of job performance.)
Kentucky	None	None	None
Louisiana	None	None	Limited law. (Random testing allowed for public employees in safety-sensitive positions. Private employees subject to procedural protections.)
Maine	None	None	Good law. (Probable cause is required unless a position is safety sensitive.)
Maryland	None	None	None for private employees. Good law for public employees. (Particularized probable cause is needed for most categories of State employees.)
Massachusetts	None	None	None
Michigan	None	None	None

State	Electronic Monitoring	Genetic Testing	Urine Testing
Minnesota	None	None	Good law. (Only employees in safety-sensitive positions may be randomly tested.)
Mississippi	None	None	Limited law. (Procedural requirements only.)
Missouri	None	None	None
Montana	None	None	Good law. (No random testing.)
Nebraska	None	None	Limited law. (Procedural requirements only.)
Nevada	None	None	None for private employees. Good law for public employees. (State employees are subject to a reasonable belief standard, unless the position is safety-sensitive. Applicants for safety sensitive positions must be tested.)
New Hampshire	None	Genetic law	None
New Jersey	None	None	None
New Mexico	None	None	None
New York	None	Genetic law	None
North Carolina	None	None	Limited law. (Procedural requirements only.)
North Dakota	None	None	None
Ohio	None	None	None
Oklahoma	None	None	Limited law. (Procedural requirements only.)
Oregon	None	Genetic law	None
Pennsylvania	None	None	None
Rhode Island	None	Genetic law	Limited law - Good law. (Reasonable cause is needed for employees, but not for applicants with conditional job offers.)
South Carolina	None	None	None for private employees. Good law for public employees. (Reasonable suspicion is needed for employees in safety-sensitive government positions
Tennessee	None	None	None for private employees. Limited law for public employees. (Corrections employees can be randomly tested.)
Texas	None	None	None for private employees. There may be state constitutional protection for public employees, however, the legal status of this is unclear.
Utah	None	None	Limited law. (Procedural requirements only.)
Vermont	None	None	Good law. (Probable cause is needed to test any employee. Job applicants can be tested under very limited circumstances.)
Virginia	None	None	None
Washington	None	None	None
West Virginia	None	None	None
Wisconsin	None	Genetic law	None
Wyoming	None	None	None

KEY

Genetic Law = state laws exist prohibiting employers from requiring genetic tests or using genetic health predictions in employment decisions.

None = There is no state law concerning this issue.

Limited Law = A law exists providing some protection in this area.

Good Law = The state has an acceptable law concerning this issue.

This table provides information on the status of workplace privacy laws, state by state, as of August, 1996.

We Have Your Number[4]

The Rush for a National ID Card

The U.S. Commission on Immigration Reform, headed by widely respected former Texas Congresswoman Barbara Jordan, turned in its long-awaited recommendations in September, and among them was one that could severely curb traditional American freedoms.

Reacting to mounting national concern—even hysteria—over illegal immigration, the Commission proposed establishing a Federal employment-eligibility database to discourage the hiring of illegals. The file, based on Social Security numbers and information provided by the Immigration and Naturalization Service, would contain the identities of all persons authorized to reside and work in the United States.

The suggestion was warmly received by the media and many members of Congress, though it invites the nation to cross a treacherous threshold by instituting identity-authentication technologies that could easily be marshaled as an apparatus of repression.

The idea of a national system of mass surveillance has always been rejected in the United States as fundamentally at odds with the ideals of a free society. But the "emergency" of illegal immigration provides an opportunity to manipulate popular opinion and the will of Congress to support a fraud-proof identity-authentication scheme.

Employers would be required to query the new Federal database to verify whether a job applicant is authorized to work in the United States. Supposedly, this would neutralize the "job magnet" by making it impossible for illegal immigrants to work in this country.

Any such system would require an identifying token—an ID card. In an early draft circulated last fall, the Commission explicitly called for issuing such cards to all Americans. In its latest version, the report merely recognized that some sort of identifying token would be necessary to make the system work.

The proposal has not been welcomed by minority-rights and civil-liberties groups. Cecilia Munoz, a senior policy analyst with the National Council of La Raza, a national Latino advocacy organization, says the most immediate threat of an identity-card system—no matter how or when it is instituted—is that it could become a tool of State-sponsored control or harassment of minorities.

---

[4] Article by Peter Cassidy, writer from Boston about white-collar crime, technology, and national affairs, from *The Progressive* 58:28-9 D '94. Copyright © 1994 Peter F. Cassidy. Reprinted with permission.

"What we're talking about is a de-facto national ID card for minorities, for Latinos, or Asians, or anyone who looks or talks differently," she says.

But the Clinton Administration's reaction when the Jordan Commission submitted its official recommendations to the Senate Subcommittee on Immigration and Alien Affairs was not to reject the proposal on ideological or civil-liberties grounds. In principle, the Administration favors high-tech identity-authentication technologies such as fraud-proof ID cards, so the Administration's public criticism of the Commission's recommendation was not that it would impart draconian powers to the State, but that available Government information to create such a database is not yet accurate enough.

Many Government agencies stand to gain from the development of high-tech snoopery. Sitting on the Administration's Information Infrastructure Task Force, for example, are representatives of the Internal Revenue Service, which only recently was rocked by disclosures that some of its agents had been selling information stolen from IRS files, and of the National Security Agency, which has been used by several Administrations as an instrument of political surveillance and repression. These agencies and others engaged in law enforcement or espionage would be the ultimate beneficiaries of a national identity-authentication system that would survive long after concerns about immigration had given way to some other real or imagined crisis.

"The funny thing about this is that everyone I know in Government understands what is happening and they don't like it personally," says William Murray, a consultant on information security at Deloitte & Touche, a national accounting and business-management consulting firm.

"The people I know at the National Institute of Standards and Technology and at the NSA are not in favor of any of these things," Murray told me in a telephone interview. "They're not proud of it; they feel they have no personal control over it. Many of them feel victimized. They don't like their jobs—but they think the institutional agenda is too powerful. They can't wait to retire to become whistleblowers."

For a long time, the political dialogue over national ID cards has closely accompanied debates over immigration policy. Most immigration-control bills that Congress considered during the 1980s included a mandate for a national ID-card system, but none ever made it into law, though it came close in the 1990 Immigration Act; an ID-card provision of that legislation was killed by the Congressional Hispanic caucus, according to David Banisar, an analyst with the Electronic Privacy Information Center, a public-interest research organization that focuses on emerging privacy issues.

Each immigration-reform act has, however, added new elements to the technology of privacy invasion. The Immigration Act of 1986, for example, compelled parents to register their children for a Social Security number before they were even toddlers.

During the 1980s, champions of identity-authentication technologies proliferated throughout the Federal bureaucracy. The State Department advocated replacing paper passports with machine-scannable tokens. However, actually instituting any of the proposed systems turned out to be difficult. President Reagan was opposed on ideological grounds, and his successor, George Bush, showed no interest in reversing Reagan's position.

The Clinton Administration came to power as an activist government with an appreciation of the potential of information technologies. During the 1992 Presidential race, Clinton aides talked openly of establishing a centralized, national medical data system to reduce health-care administrative costs. According to the Los Angeles Times, Clinton policy analyst Ira Magaziner said, "We want to create an integrated system with a card that everyone will get at birth."

"...Clinton aides talked openly of establishing a centralized, national medical data system..."

Vice President Al Gore's "reinventing government" initiative is, at its core, a discourse on the role of information technology in systematizing government to work better and deliver services more efficiently. But how to make all that happen without establishing a national identity-authentication system is, given the available technologies, an almost impossible assignment.

Existing information technologies are already being harnessed for surveillance purposes. State human-services and law-enforcement agencies are using Social Security numbers and state tax department data to track down dead-beat fathers who have stopped paying child support. This kind of tracking program is, in itself, a telling example of how information technologies can end up being marshaled for entirely different purposes than those for which they were intended. When the Social Security Act was passed in 1935, Americans were promised that Social Security numbers would never be used by any agency except the Social Security Administration or for any purpose other than old-age pension records.

ID cards are already being surpassed for accuracy and security by biometric measurement systems. Instead of issuing a card, an identity-authenticating system might scan an individual's thumb or record his or her DNA. The INS is now testing a passport-replacement program called the Passenger Accelerated Service System (INS Pass) that can authenticate travelers' identities at customs by scanning the shape of a traveler's hand while it is pressed on a biometric reading plate at the customs gate. The system, reported to be almost perfectly accurate, now serves about 20,000 frequent fliers who, no doubt, revel in its convenience.

The Defense Department is issuing its new Multi-Technology Automated Reader Card (MARC) to U.S. military personnel through a program developed by the Pentagon's Information Technology Board. Credit-card-sized MARC tokens carry an integrated-circuit chip and bar code. Members of the armed forces use it for such onbase services as meals and medical care.

If such technology finds acceptance at the same speed that urine-testing for drug abuse did, Americans could be carrying national ID cards in a decade or two. Urinalysis was begun in the Navy in 1973 when the first testing kits were perfected. In 1986, President Reagan signed an executive order mandating urinalysis for civilian employees of military agencies. Now, urinalysis is a permanent fixture of industrial life in the United States.

A full-blown national ID card like the military's MARC system could only find popular support, however, in the emotional politics of the drug—or immigration—"crisis." As Senator Alan Simpson of Wyoming, a perennial sponsor of immigration-reform legislation that would institute a national ID system, said during one hearing this year, "We don't do anything logically, steadily. We do things out of political pressure."

Identity-authentication technologies will inevitably become cheaper, faster, more accurate, and more attractive as a means of surveillance and control. In an economy of constant job mobility, no more important management tool could be devised than an employment-eligibility database that would have to be queried when an applicant seeks employment.

But the consequences of allowing Federal agencies to take this course will be development of state-sponsored surveillance technologies and the loss of privacy. Establishment of the Jordan Commission's database is not a step that should be taken in haste, fear, or anger—all of which have characterized the debate on illegal immigration. Posterity may reverse this generation's attitude toward immigrants, but by then the power conferred on the State to intrude on the lives of the citizenry will probably be irreversible. We will have laid the foundation of a police state— a place where it will be technically impossible to protect oneself from warrantless searches or lose oneself in the crowd.

"In an economy of constant job mobility, no more important management tool could be devised than an employment-eligibility database..."

Workplace Privacy:
Issues and Implications[5]

Some companies have mounted cameras to oversee employees suspected of crime; others have installed electronic devices to eavesdrop on phone calls.

Privacy in the workplace always has been controversial, but interest has been heightened in recent years by increasingly sophisticated means of conducting random drug tests, background checks, and electronic performance monitoring. While the significance of workplace privacy has increased, so has its politics, making this issue one of particular importance and sensitivity in corporate America.

In a study conducted by the Society for Human Resource Management (SHRM), human resource professionals most consistently favored the use of drug and alcohol testing, soliciting criminal records checks, and monitoring visual display terminal (VDT) keystrokes and phone activity. While employers may deem these activities as essential to preserve workplace safety and productivity, many employees would argue that they violate their privacy, both on the job and at home.

What if work performance is impeded by personal interests or other activities, however? Employer advocates maintain that companies have the right to hire the best-qualified individual for the job and exercise certain expectations of that person. They also argue that they have a right and a responsibility to protect legitimate business interests through quality control, workplace safety, and health care cost containment.

Few would dispute that employers have certain rights and responsibilities, but at what cost to the personal rights of their workers? The boundaries delineating acceptable and unacceptable intervention into an employee's private life are being expanded rapidly. Many privacy rights activists fear that the list of unacceptable habits, hobbies, or health conditions soon will be fair game in the office.

For example, smoking in the workplace has been banned in many organizations, particularly as a result of recent studies that revealed the dangers of secondhand smoke, but should employers have the right to prohibit smoking at home, too? There is a proven corollary between smoking and the likelihood of developing serious (and costly) diseases, and employers consider those who smoke at all to be so sufficiently at-risk that they are advocating a right to recourse.

---

[5] Article by Michael Losey, president and CEO, Society for Human Resources Management, Alexandria, from *USA Today* 123:76-8 S '94. Copyright © 1994 *USA Today*. Reprinted with permission.

In the SHRM Privacy in the Workplace survey, 77% of the human resource professionals who responded endorsed a company's right to establish health care differentials in the insurance premiums of those who smoke. Employee advocates worry that this may enable employers to test for cholesterol, hypertension, or even genetic anomalies.

Workers' fears regarding the future of testing may not be unfounded. In 1993, the municipal government of Athens, Ga., proposed that every job applicant be administered a cholesterol test, eliminating those whose levels ranked in the highest 20%. When a vehement local outcry ensued, the policy was abandoned. While the proposal was axed, it still serves to illustrate the length to which some employers have attempted to extend testing.

Drug testing still is divisive, but now widely accepted as a means of maintaining workplace safety and productivity standards. Yet, alcohol, though legally and socially acceptable, is a drug capable of impairing job performance, and some companies already prohibit its off-site consumption.

"Performance tests would offer more privacy to the worker and promote a less accusatory response by employers."

In Indiana, an employee was terminated when he volunteered that he occasionally drank socially in his off hours, a violation of company policy. The Indiana Court of Appeals ruled that the firm could not demonstrate that his drinking had a negative impact on his work performance or there was just cause for termination.

The court indicated that employers may regulate a worker's conduct on the job, but "the same interest does not always exist in regulating the employee's off-duty conduct." While the court ruled in the worker's favor, the language was vague and does not preclude the possibility that this policy might be valid under different circumstances.

Thanks to technological advances, impairment of any kind soon may be detected by computer. Called performance or impairment testing by its creators, a game-like device has been developed that can test judgment and motor coordination through the ability to manipulate a cursor on a VDT screen.

The benefit of this type of screening is that it is less invasive than urinalysis and would not reveal the cause of any employee impairment. Performance tests would offer more privacy to the worker and promote a less accusatory response by employers. They are being touted by both civil libertarians and employer rights advocates as a way of killing two birds with one stone— the tests can detect problems, but diffuse hostility in the process of determining and correcting the cause of the impairment.

Other technological advances are not being received nearly so well. Many employees don't like the fact that their boss can monitor the number and speed of a data entry operator's keystrokes. Some companies have mounted tiny fish-eye cameras to oversee employees suspected of crime, and others have installed electronic listening devices that can eavesdrop on employee phone calls, as well as record the number, frequency, and destination of such calls.

One of the most controversial developments is the "active badge." A small card that looks like an identification badge is clipped onto the worker's clothing, transmitting an infrared signal every 10 seconds to a central tracking computer.

Some critics foresee that companies will use the badges for electronic surveillance. They worry that every trip to the bathroom or time spent at the water cooler will be scrutinized. Proponents say the devices will allow workers to make more efficient use of their time. The badges will tell supervisors exactly where an employee is located in the building, eliminating the need to hunt down workers. Calls could be patched to the nearest phone when an employee is away from his or her desk.

The active badge still is in the fine-tuning stages, but employer and employee advocates already are grappling with the implications. For instance, a manager with a grudge could abuse the system. Nevertheless, employers are convinced that, with ethical implementation, the badges could be a breakthrough in workplace management.

Electronic "Spying"

Another of the more controversial issues in the debate over employee rights is that of electronic monitoring and surveillance. The subject has acquired a high media profile and often is perceived as sinister, an Orwellian prophecy fulfilled. In fact, electronic monitoring is not that new. It has been utilized in the manufacturing industry for many years to track output, inventory, and general efficiency.

Management argues that sophisticated technology merely enables the company to supervise its staff more effectively, but many employees disagree. They maintain that this less conspicuous form of old-fashioned human supervision makes them nervous and implies mistrust. Privacy advocates claim that workers are less productive, and the effect on morale also has been called into question.

"Privacy advocates claim that workers are less productive, and the effect on morale also has been called into question."

Of course, one could argue that there are many good reasons to monitor employees. A number of recent court cases have made employers legally liable for their workers' negligent or criminal behavior. Corporate espionage and workplace theft is on the rise and, while most employers utilize electronic monitoring judiciously—and only when a problem is suspected—employees remain skeptical.

Worker grievances are especially significant today due to the changes that have affected the employer-employee relationship. For most of the post-World War II period, workplace issues were dominated by blue-collar concerns and addressed by organized labor unions in negotiation with management. However, union membership has eroded considerably, and the nation's workforce now is dominated by white-collar concerns.

Because of union decline and other changing conditions, a vacuum exists in the balance of power between employers and employees. A critical factor shaping the social contract between management and workers has been the emergence of government establishing employment policies and conditions. Moreover, lawyers increasingly are becoming the primary mouthpiece of the American workforce, and employee grievances now are being settled in the courtroom.

Consider the case of Sibi Soroka, who was administered a three-hour, 700-question battery of psychological tests when he applied for a security guard's position at a national discount retailer. Soroka was offered the job, but complained he was "humiliated" and "embarrassed" by some of the questions. Among the statements of which he was asked to agree or disagree were "I have no difficulty in starting or holding my bowel movement" and "I would like to be a florist."

"Smoking, drinking, and obesity could be determined to be addictions over which individuals have no control."

Soroka and several other applicants filed suit and won the case before a California court of appeals. The court ruled that the company failed to show that the test was sufficiently relevant to the job, and it barred further use unless a "compelling interest" could be demonstrated. The state's supreme court was reviewing the lawsuit when the retailer settled out of court with the plaintiffs for $1,300,000.

In another case, a payroll clerk in Indiana lost her job when traces of nicotine were detected during a company-mandated urinalysis. The clerk filed suit, even though the firm had an acknowledged policy of terminating those who smoke outside the workplace. While she didn't get her job back, the incident did rally privacy proponents, and Indiana now has a law on the books protecting those who smoke off the job.

Litigation is a piecemeal approach to a matter that is growing in importance and complexity. Employers can't afford to postpone consideration of privacy issues until they personally are confronted by a difficult situation. By that time, the company may find its policy dictated by a court.

The increasing rule of Federal legislation undoubtedly will play a prominent role in the privacy debate. The Americans with Disabilities Act (ADA) frequently is interpreted more broadly than many in management might prefer. While the ADA doesn't explicitly protect lifestyles or behaviors, their negative effects could be ruled a disability. Smoking, drinking, and obesity could be determined to be addictions over which individuals have no control. Since high cholesterol and hypertension can be inherited, consideration of those conditions when hiring, promoting, or otherwise evaluating an employee could be prohibited.

The ADA states that employers only can deny employment to those who are unable to perform a job due to prohibitive physical or mental limitations and when that job can not be accommodated to a worker's disabilities. For instance, an individual can't be denied employment because he or she can't fit into a desk or stand tall enough to see over a counter. Neither is the threat a worker may pose to health care costs a valid reason to deny or terminate employment.

Legislation is being considered regarding electronic monitoring. The Privacy for Consumer and Workers Act (H.R. 1900) proposes a three-tier approach to restrict employee surveillance: new hires could be subject to random and continuous monitoring; those employed more than 60 days, but less than five years, could be subject to limited monitoring; and management would be restricted from engaging in monitoring workers who have been on the job for more than five years, unless it has "reasonable suspicion" that the individual is involved in criminal or other behavior that "adversely affects the employer's interests."

The legislation also calls for employers to provide prior written notification explaining when the monitoring will occur, what methods will be used, and how the information gathered will be utilized to determine work performance. Additionally, companies must notify prospective employees of the practice during the first interview. These protections are sought primarily by white-collar workers in a white-collar workforce. Yet, employers still need to ensure that white-collar productivity is audited every bit as much as when stopwatch and time-and-motion studies were conducted on the blue-collar workers of yesterday.

"The Privacy for Consumer and Workers Act (H.R. 1900) proposes a three-tier approach to restrict employee surveillance..."

The Society for Human Resource Management opposes any such legislation that attempts to regulate, restrict, or interfere with a company's legitimate means for assessing job performance. SHRM does support the practice of notifying workers of all employment practices, including electronic monitoring, at the time a job offer is made and at regular intervals thereafter.

In the SHRM privacy survey, respondents were generally in favor of a company's right to monitor its employees. About 60% supported monitoring VDT keystrokes, almost 50% endorsed recording employee phone activity, and nearly 40% agreed that employers have a right to monitor their workers with video equipment.

Unawareness of Regulations

The study also revealed, however, that an alarming disparity exists between corporate interest in workplace privacy issues and understanding of the laws and regulations pertaining to those issues. More than 50% of the respondents did not know if there were any state laws affecting employee surveillance or records disclosure. One third were unaware of regulations affecting the collection of employee information, workers' access to their own files, or substance abuse testing. This deficiency, coupled with the fear of litigation, promotes a great deal of apprehension among employers and is a marked contrast to the increasingly popular perception that they are eager to implement progressively more invasive policies.

Many employers are unfamiliar with laws pertaining to worker privacy. Because advocates of employee rights likely will be diligent in pursuing more statutory protection, workers probably will be successful in securing some degree of regulation in regard to privacy. While various laws and court rulings are intended to clarify and define the lines between legitimate employee and employer rights, they have created a number of unknowns. The result is a flurry of ill-defined and contradictory state laws that seem to impede, rather than facilitate, corporate policy-making.

In a May, 1992, article for *HR Magazine*, Rebecca Grant, assistant professor of infomation systems, University of Cincinnati, offered several suggestions to help managers cope with sensitive privacy issues:

—Choose tasks deliberately. Some behaviors such as being courteous to customers simply do not lend themselves to quantitative measurement or numeric surrogates. Employees find monitors most tolerable if they are directed at tasks they feel are important and can be reflected accurately in quantitative terms.

—Monitor regularly. Most work is input-driven. A salesclerk only can sell to customers who are in the store, and a telephone operator only is able to respond to incoming calls. Workloads vary from day to day, and everyone is prone to the occasional "bad day." For these reasons, intermittent monitoring may not reflect fairly an individual's most consistent job performance.

—Supplement monitoring with data on work quality. It is not as easy to describe or evaluate less tangible aspects of performance. Yet, it is vital to have a measurement system that gets regular, visible use. Employees should be told about the quality of their work as often as they read or hear about their production.

—Provide a mechanism for employee participation and error correction. Explain what sort of monitoring will be conducted, when, and for what purpose. Workers need to know that the monitoring is fair, accurate, and complete. They also should be allowed to review information collected about them and to challenge it effectively.

—Keep monitoring in perspective. A properly designed and executed program usually will be more accurate and consistent than human observation alone. However, there still is great value in human interaction when evaluating workplace productivity. Listening to employee and customer opinions always will be a valuable resource in such assessments.

The next few years likely will see more effort to enact or expand workplace privacy laws. Today's workers are less inclined than ever before to comply blindly with "company policy," so managers would be well-advised to anticipate and plan accordingly. Every effort should be made by employers and employees alike to cooperate in recognizing the rights and responsibilities inherent in a productive workplace relationship. With honest communication and thoughtful preparation, management and labor can reach a balance that is mutually beneficial.

"Every effort should be made by employers and employees alike to cooperate in recognizing the rights and responsibilities..."

III. Privacy and Medical Records

Editor's Introduction

Section Three begins with letters to the editor of *The Wall Street Journal* written in response to a previous article which remarked that the Health-Insurance Portability and Accountability Act, made law August of 1996, poses a serious threat to medical record confidentiality. The law includes an "Administrative Simplification" amendment which would require the creation of a massive medical record data bank. According to these letters, it is feared that such a data bank can be easily accessed and patient medical records will be distributed without the knowledge of the patient.

The following article by Don E. Detmer and James Love in *Business and Health* addresses the issue of the Medical Records Confidentiality Act [the Bennett/Leahy Bill (S. 1360)] presently being reworked, with Detmer arguing in its favor, and Love arguing against. Detmer maintains that the act would bring uniformity to the handling of medical records from state to state; provide more patient access to the records; and allow access chiefly to governmental agencies and the medical profession. Love, on the other hand, maintains that companies, not just governmental agencies and the medical profession, would have no difficulty in obtaining the medical records; that all personal identifiers in the records would be intact; and that the act would pose an obvious invasion of privacy rights.

The following article, from *Consumer Reports*, discusses the possible parties that can achieve access to your medical records and what you can do to prevent such access. According to this article, as records become easily transferable files, opportunities to view those files grow. In response the patient must become increasingly aware of what he or she discloses to their doctor.

In a related article on the Medical Records Confidentiality Act, Christine Gorman, in *Time* magazine, comments that medical records contain some of the most sensitive personal information about patients—including sexual orientation, past drug use, and genetic predisposition to various diseases—and ought to be strictly sheltered from outside access. Gorman also points out that the health information industry is now a $40 billion business.

Nat Hentoff in an article in *The Progressive* brings up another medical record issue—that of whether to reveal the presence of HIV antibodies in infants when testing newborn infants for various other diseases. Doing so, civil rights advocates argue, would instantly identify the mother as having AIDS and make her vulnerable to discrimination and stigmatization. Hentoff, on the other hand, believes that the welfare of the baby must be a primary consideration. A bill to require disclosure was introduced in the New York State legislature in 1994. It was defeated. One of its supporters, however, was George Pataki, now New York's governor, and the case for the disclosure of medical records of this kind is still far from over.

Don E. Detmer and Elaine B. Steen, in an article in *Issues in Science and Technology*, discuss the debate about individual rights threatening to derail the implementation of a much-needed federal policy for protecting personal health data. The lack of a sound and consistent policy framework has prompted Congress to consider providing federal legal protection, however, no legislation to that end has been passed.

Predictive genetic testing for diseases may improve medical care, but human rights could be overlooked in the process. The final article from *USA Today* examines the host of complex social and ethical issues raised by the subject of genetic testing. According to this article, great care must be exercised in the development of public policies so that people are protected from the type of discrimination genetic testing could potentially cause.

Letters to the Editor: The End of Personal Medical Privacy[1]

Dr. Jane Orient's May 30 editorial-page article sounds the alarm about the criminalization of medicine and its danger for patients who may lose the last bastion of privacy in medical practice, the independent practitioner. 'Administrative Simplification,' one of the amendments, which Dr. Orient says is included in the insurance reform bill that passed in the House, is not a part of the Kassebaum-Kennedy version that unanimously passed the Senate.

The senators wisely left this section out, recognizing it would be a death knell to medical privacy. It would give the green light to the computerization and development of a birth-to-grave medical record on every American without their knowledge or consent. There is a lot of pressure, however, to include this amendment in the final version of the bill when the conferees meet. If this happens it will be a disaster for the longstanding tradition of doctor/patient confidentiality and personal privacy, and will be a high price to pay for even modest insurance reform.

"The traditional right of medical privacy is being eroded...."

We are far away from solving the problem posed by the availability or affordability of health care. But while that debate rages on, this other 'quiet crisis' has begun to surface. The traditional right of medical privacy is being eroded as our medical records become transformed into commodities desired by insurers, employers, researchers, and yes, even police.

Consider a few recent examples:
—A woman with average computer skills accessed information about her psychiatric condition from her insurance company's database. Concerned that future employers could obtain it as easily as she had, she requested its removal. She was turned down.
—Boston clinicians who had promised AIDS patients absolute confidentiality were shocked when federal auditors demanded to see patients' names in the records. The auditors then shared this information with other agencies.
—Maryland has begun collecting information for a state database authorized to track every doctor-patient encounter — even psychotherapy sessions — without patient consent. The state is authorized to demand reporting of this information even if you pay 'out-of-pocket.'

---

[1] Article from *The Wall Street Journal* A 13 Je 7, '96. Copyright © 1996 Dow Jones & Company, Inc. Reprinted with permission. All rights reserved.

There are powerful interests working to ensure the free flow of medical information. In fact, the Senate Labor and Human Resources Committee is expected to vote soon on a bill that would ride roughshod over states that try to protect the medical privacy of their inhabitants. This bill, S. 1360, masquerades as privacy legislation, but it creates the ability to develop national and regional health databases without requiring the consent of the people whose most intimate details would become widely available—the patients. The bill contains a great many exceptions to the rule of informed consent.

Health-care entities have invested heavily in the creation of the computerized medical record. More than any other innovation, the electronic record is touted as the cost-cutting measure that will eliminate so many of the burdensome tasks of paper-pushing. What is not considered is the way in which patient care will be forever changed, or how it will affect the ability of patients to control some of the most intimate data collected about them.

People still erroneously believe that their conversations with their doctors are protected by the Hippocratic Oath—'Whatever in connection with my professional practice, I see or hear in the life of men which ought not to be spoken of abroad, I will not divulge, as reckoning that all such should be kept secret.' The principle has served as the bedrock of good health care, because only when we feel free to speak candidly will we reveal the information that can help doctors to diagnose and treat us.

No one has ever said that the Hippocratic Oath is defunct, but current practices have made it so. Stories about the collection of psychiatric and other clinical notes by insurance companies, employers and HMOs abound. Even now, once such confidences are collected, they are banked in a centralized database for future use when you switch insurers, jobs, or apply for life or disability insurance. Your medical history has been transformed from a healing tool in the hands of doctors to a weapon of Big Brother, who will decide whether you're too sick to be employed or insured.

President Clinton's health-care proposal, now discredited, contained a scheme which would have required all medical information collected about every American to be deposited into a national database. Such widespread data gathering would be tantamount to mounting a video camera in every examining room in the country. While the Clinton plan has died, its surveillance provisions live on in the House version of the insurance reform legislation—the so-called 'Administrative Simplification' provisions.

On May 16, Rep. James McDermott (D., Wash.), a psychiatrist, introduced the first medical privacy bill that truly focuses on the patient as the center of health-information systems. This bill offers strong protection for all medical information, especially the results of genetic testing.

States' rights, individual freedom, and our belief that we have a right to privacy will be in jeopardy if the bill currently before the Senate passes. There will be no cost savings when people delay or forgo necessary treatment because they are not ready to face the klieg lights of the examining room.

Denise M. Nagel, M.D.
A.G. Breitenstein
Boston

(Dr. Nagel is president of Coalition for Patient Rights of New England and Mr. Breitenstein is director of the Justice Resource Institute and the Health Law Institute.)

Dr. Orient leaves the impression that provisions added to my health insurance reform bill to fight fraud and abuse are part of some secret and sinister plot to drive innocent doctors out of business. These mischaracterizations simply have no basis in fact.

> *"...the provisions are focused on penalizing serious, organized, intentional theft and fraud."*

Health-care fraud and abuse currently consume an estimated 10% of U.S. health-care spending, according to the General Accounting Office. That's $90 billion a year that goes to those stealing from the system rather than toward increasing treatment and coverage.

The fraud and abuse provisions, which were part of a broader package added to my targeted health insurance reform bill by Sens. Dole and Roth, are not intended to punish doctors for innocent mistakes or omissions, as Dr. Orient implies. In fact, doctors are expressly protected from such oversights. Instead, the provisions are focused on penalizing serious, organized, intentional theft and fraud.

Dr. Orient further suggests that the fraud and abuse provisions were slipped into the bill without serious consideration. In fact, they were based on recommendations from a 1993 report by a task force organized by the Bush administration. They have been thoroughly debated and were passed twice already by this Congress as part of the Republican's balanced budget act. Moreover, the provisions substantially mirror existing fraud statutes designed to give enforcement authorities more precise tools to protect consumers against health-care fraud and abuse. It should be noted that Dr. Orient offers no alternative for dealing with this serious problem.

The common-sense health insurance reform bill currently working its way through Congress enjoys the enthusiastic support of the American Medical Association and 44 of the nation's medical specialty societies. The fraud and abuse provisions strengthen that bill and merit serious consideration despite Dr. Orient's exaggerated claims.

Sen. Nancy Landon Kassebaum
(R., Kan.)
Washington

Dr. Orient's article was disturbing for many reasons. Legislation that conceivably could subject well-intentioned physicians to criminal penalties for inadvertent and innocent coding and billing errors is outrageous and will not pass constitutional muster, even if it passes Congress (which isn't likely).

The House and Senate health-care reform bills both contain antifraud amendments. The Senate version includes a 'knowing and willful' intent standard that should ensure that honest mistakes do not result in criminal liability. The House language is more ambiguous, and must be corrected. We have presented the conferees with amendments to solve the problem.

There is a problem with health-care fraud in this country. The health-care 'industry' has become a haven for entrepreneurs, and some are not honest. According to the FBI, physicians are the least likely segment of the system to be involved in fraud, but they do see it. Our primary effort has been to get more doctors to report it. Heavy-handed and insensitive legislation that could criminalize innocent conduct only makes the problem worse.

Lonnie R. Bristow, M.D.
President
American Medical Association
Chicago

Who Should Have Access to Your Medical Record?[2]

Mid-autumn of last year [1995] saw the introduction in the Senate of the Medical Records Confidentiality Act. Recognizing the impact of storing thousands upon thousands of individual medical records in computerized data banks, the Bennett/Leahy Bill (S. 1360) would establish uniform federal rules for use and disclosure. Critics argue that the proposed rules would allow corporations to paw through personal records and dangerously broaden access for law enforcement and other government officials. Arguing in favor of the bill on these pages is Don E. Detmer, MD, senior vice president at the University of Virginia in Charlottesville. Opposition is voiced by James Love, director of the Consumer Project on Technology, which is part of the Center for Responsive Law in Washington, D.C.

Good Health Care Is Built On Good Data
By Don E. Detmer, MD

The Information Age is upon us all, and the impact can be readily observed in health care, where the emerging technology of computer-based patient records is beginning to improve care in terms of both results and costs. Traditional paper medical records are typically incomplete and often illegible or inaccessible at key moments. Physicians caring for the injured and ill need relevant and timely information. In an era of powerful medications and a growing variety of artificial body parts, having data on past care can mean the difference between life and death, whether the patient is a familiar face or total stranger.

Many, if not all, Americans believe their personal health data should be confidential and that existing laws give them adequate protection. The reality is that no national law adequately secures the privacy and integrity of personal health information. Neither, in many states, are citizens assured the sensible and important right of access to their medical records so that they may amend inaccuracies. Such gaps have existed for many years, and now the evolution of technology is forcing us to confront the issues and develop laws to keep pace.

In 1991 and again in 1995, the Institute of Medicine of the National Academy of Sciences urged national legislation to overcome contradictions among state laws so that people who live in one state, work in another and have insurance in a third can get their care. If a sensible law is not passed soon, more states will add their strands to a tangled and costly web of laws that will

"The reality is that no national law adequately secures the privacy and integrity of personal health information."

[2] Article by Don E. Detmer, MD, senior vice president of the University of Virginia, and James Love, director of the Consumer Report on Technology at the center for Representative Law in Washington, D.C. from *Business & Health* 14:59-60 F '96. Copyright © 1996 *Business & Health*. Reprinted with permission.

take years to resolve.

The Bennett/Leahy bill, with a few desirable amendments, will create a law that addresses these significant issues. This legislation relates directly to trust within the doctor-patient relationship, which has been eroded in recent years by numerous social forces. Every person must know that his or her personal information is important and respected. Patients need assurance that they can speak honestly with their caregiver without fear of later, inappropriate use of what they reveal. That is why S. 1360 puts those who handle personal health data on notice that they have a trust and face substantial sanctions should they willfully break that trust. The bill wisely allows for a few carefully specified exceptions to the patient's desire for absolute confidentiality, including public health, law enforcement and medical research.

"Privacy is a good, but it is one of a number of competing goods that must be balanced."

The last of those three is particularly important as we enter an era of major advances in medical care. To foreclose the ability to offer the benefits of research to the entire community because some individuals wish to exempt their data from scientific analysis would hold the entire society hostage. Just as immunizations protect us only if a sufficient percentage of the population is immunized, so too does the success of health research depend on sufficient participation. Privacy is a good, but it is one of a number of competing goods that must be balanced. As Thomas Jefferson said, "Without health, there can be no happiness. An attention to health, therefore, should come before all other objects."

A large number of citizen advocacy groups, health professional organizations and able senators of both political parties support this legislation. All health professionals and those in health-related businesses have a responsibility to get behind it to assure that health data are used solely for the purposes for which they are collected and to make sure that those individuals who abuse this responsibility are held liable. A desire for perfect legislation or continued study must not prevent putting good safeguards in place now. As the Information Age matures, our laws must mature with it.

Privacy Protection or Legalized Prowling
By James Love

Congress is addressing the question of privacy for medical records, and the major bill, introduced in October, was originally expected to sail through the Senate. The principal sponsors, Republicans Robert Bennett of Utah and Patrick Leahy of Vermont, seem fired up about the issue, and the list of co-sponsors forms a who's who of the Senate leadership. This includes the Senate President and Senate Minority Leader and the Chair and Ranking Minority member of the Senate Committee on Labor and Human Resources plus about a dozen others. The initial hearings on the bill featured nine supporters and only a single opponent. Nevertheless, doubts about the legislation have grown as consumers have examined it more carefully.

S. 1360 is titled the "Medical Records Confidentiality Act," but it reads more like the "Medical Records Access Act." The bill seeks "to ensure personal privacy," but it allows a host of "other purposes" that are mostly about granting millions of persons access to your medical records without your consent and often without any notice. Who would have these broad rights?

Companies like Equifax or TRW could obtain your records, without your knowledge, and make them available to any number of third parties without your consent. The firm could do this as a federally regulated "Health Information Service" or simply as one of many contractors for other "health care trustees" such as your insurance company.

Medical researchers, including those who work for profit-making accounting firms, could obtain your records, with virtually all personal identifiers intact. There isn't any real incentive for researchers to invest in "blinding" the data.

Public health officials from just about any city or state qualify for access to all your records.

You work for an insurance company? No problem, just get "consent." You know, as in, anybody who wants to process a claim has to sign away his confidentiality.

Employers or schools? Well, be careful about the Americans for Disabilities Act, but yeah, you get everything you want, too.

Law enforcement officials? No need for consent, as long as the information is thought to be "relevant" to an investigation. Suppose a local deputy sheriff wants to search for records on a person whose identify is unknown. Serve a warrant or subpoena? On whom? Let's see, that one looks familiar. Oh excuse me, that's not the individual I'm looking for, let me try another.

I'm not making this up. S. 1360 anticipates all of these types of access to your medical records.

Supporters say the bill simply recognizes the reality that people lost their medical records privacy 20 years ago. You can't get it back, you can only make the process a bit more manageable. Of course, to make things more manageable, S. 1360 takes away your right to sue for invasion of privacy under common law and pre-empts a wide range of state laws. No wonder the medical records industry is so excited about the bill.

What really needs to be done? Here are a few of the suggestions that consumer groups are making:

Protect consumers from giving "consent" for access to records under coercion.

Prevent health insurance companies from sharing identified records with third parties.

Require tougher notice and warrant requirements for the millions of government officials who want access to your records.

Provide special protections for mental health, genetic and other especially sensitive information.

Set a federal floor on privacy, not a ceiling.

"...S. 1360 takes away your right to sue for invasion of privacy under common law...."

Do we need a federal medical records privacy bill? Well, maybe, but certainly not a bill that purports to give privacy and doesn't deliver.

Who's Reading Your Medical Records?[3]

In 1992, the New York Congressional campaign of Nydia M. Velazquez was shaken when someone told New York newspapers that she had sought emergency treatment at a hospital after a suicide attempt. Despite the revelation, Velazquez won the election—and went on to sue a Manhattan hospital for $10-million for failing to protect her privacy. In other cases, medical information made public has been even more devastating. It has cost people their jobs or ruined their standing in the community.

The medical information people give their doctors and hospitals is probably the most sensitive knowledge they share with anyone outside their immediate families. It can include details about family relationships, sexual behavior, substance abuse, and, in the case of psychotherapy, even their most private thoughts. Now that information has become less secure than ever.

Until a few decades ago, no one but your doctor saw your medical records or had a reason to. But as the U.S. health-care system has become more complex, many groups have staked a claim to the information in your medical file.

Health-insurance companies require your diagnosis before they'll pay a bill. Managed-care organizations, such as HMOs, say they need medical information to monitor your treatment. Some Government benefit programs use medical records to determine your eligibility. Medical researchers often use them for large-scale studies of major diseases. Some employers, hoping to control rising medical costs, closely monitor their employees' medical treatment and health problems.

Symptoms for Sale

Medical information has become a valuable commodity that can be sold or traded. Drug companies and mailing-list brokers use the information to support giant medical mailing lists that let them target patients with specific health problems. Many private doctors now maintain computerized patient records that they make available to outside parties, such as drug companies, in return for equipment discounts. Those records may contain diagnoses of illnesses as well as prescription information.

There are no uniform legal constraints on the uses of medical records. The U.S. Constitution contains no explicit guarantee of privacy. No Federal law protects the confidentiality of medical records, although Congress may pass one soon. Some state laws prohibit certain uses of medical information, but the prohibitions

---

[3] Article by staffwriter from *Consumer Reports* 59:628-32 O '94. Copyright © 1994 Consumer Union of U.S, Inc., Yonkers, N.Y. Reprinted with permission.

and the penalties they impose vary widely.

A study on protecting medical privacy, released last fall by the Congressional Office of Technology Assessment, decried the lack of "consistent, comprehensive protection for privacy" in the present patchwork of state and Federal laws. And, in a study released earlier this year, the National Academy of Sciences' Institute of Medicine concluded that threats to medical privacy are "real and not numerically trivial."

Prying Made Easy

With the approach of health-care reform, and the continuing computerization of patient records, medical privacy is likely to become an event greater concern. When records pass electronically from doctor to hospital to pharmacy to insurance company, every stage along the way offers an opportunity for sensitive information to be misused.

"...the credit bureau Equifax found that 85 percent of those surveyed said protecting the confidentiality of medical records was absolutely essential...."

Electronic medical records are also likely to cross state lines, creating confusion over whose laws apply. The health-care industry has already begun constructing its own lanes on the information superhighway—community health information networks or CHINs—that will be used to ferry patient records.

Even today, gauging the scope of the problem is difficult. The privacy of medical records can be violated without the patient's knowledge. Even people who are aware that their records have been misused are often reluctant to go public, afraid of compounding the damage to their lives. For their part, the organizations that handle medical data tend to play down the dangers.

Still, there is good evidence that the problem is serious. The University of San Diego's Privacy Rights Clearinghouse, which educates consumers about privacy issues, has published an eye-opening list of case histories, several of which involve medical records, based on calls to its California hot line.

In a 1993 Harris poll, more than a quarter of those surveyed said that their own medical information had been improperly disclosed. It's unlikely they were being paranoid, because a comparable percentage of health-care professionals surveyed, said they knew of such violations and could describe them in detail. And those figures only cover the cases that the person involved found out about. (The same poll, commissioned by the credit bureau Equifax found that 85 percent of those surveyed said protecting the confidentiality of medical records was absolutely essential or very important in health-care reform.)

As this report went to press, Congress was considering national standards for the handling of medical information as part of health-care reform legislation. However, it would still be up to Federal regulators to make sure that any new privacy rules are enforced. If that doesn't happen, the burden for limiting the disclosure of medical information, detecting its unauthorized use, and taking action against violators will remain where it is now: on the individual consumer.

Here are some of the ways that medical information about you is collected and used, with advice on what you can do, where possible, to protect yourself.

Records in doctors' offices and hospitals were never totally secure, even before computers came along.

The handwritten notes your doctor keeps on you can be subpoenaed in court without your knowledge. And a doctor's office staff will sometimes photocopy more information than is required by a subpoena or requested by an insurance company, so unrelated medical information can be unintentionally revealed. For example, a California woman our reporter spoke with had her medical records subpoenaed after a car accident. The records mentioned a child she had given up for adoption thirty years earlier, information her doctor had written down despite her request that he not do so.

Networking Doctors' Offices

Today, your doctor's records may also be in a computer file that is accessible, without your knowledge or permission, to people outside the office. Physician Computer Network (PCN), which is partly owned by IBM, has computer access to the patient records of 41,000 doctors. That's about 1 of every 10 office-based doctors in the U.S. The firm which has been expanding rapidly in the past year by acquiring competitors, plans to reach a third of all private doctors by 1996.

PCN offers doctors computerized billing and electronic links to hospitals, labs, and insurance companies. In return, PCN requires each doctor to view promotions from drug manufacturers (which help support PCN) and reserves the right to copy patient information from the doctor's computer to its own and sell that information to other companies. According to PCN's contract with doctors, the company can collect only aggregate data and cannot identify any individual patient or doctor. A company representative told us PCN has not sold any patient information yet but may do so as early as next year once it has access to more records. That information may include patients' ages, diagnoses, treatments, and drug prescriptions. At the same time that it says it respects patients' privacy, PCN asserts that it doesn't need permission to electronically rummage through their medical records for commercial purposes.

"Physician Computer Network (PCN)...has computer access to the patient records of 41,000 doctors."

What You Can Do

While you should certainly tell your physician everything necessary for proper medical treatment, think twice before disclosing information that has no bearing on your health. As one investigator told us, "Dumb things you say in a doctor's office can end up in your file."

Ask your doctor if any part of your records can be accessed from outside the office. If they can, ask for what purpose.

Before your doctor's office sends your medical records to

another party, such as an insurance company, ask to view them for accuracy. Only about half the states guarantee patients the right to see their medical records, but many doctors will allow you to look at them as a courtesy.

Ask your doctor to notify you if your records are ever subpoenaed. Also request that only information relevant to the case be disclosed. If you've ever filled out an application for insurance, it probably contained an authorization addressed to doctors, dentists, hospitals, and other care providers similar to this one:

"I authorize you to release all medical and nonmedical information about me (the undersigned) or my children to XYZ Insurance Company, its reinsurers, and any consumer reporting agency acting for them. This authorization includes information about medical history, mental and physical condition, drug and alcohol use, and other personal information such as finances, occupation, and general reputation."

Virtually all the life-, health-, and disability-insurance policies sold in the U.S. and Canada also serve notice that a report on you may be filed with the Massachusetts-based Medical Information Bureau. The nonprofit bureau is financed and run by the insurance industry to detect fraudulent applications. It maintains records on about 15 million people, based on information provided by insurance companies.

Who's on File

Not everyone who applies for an insurance policy has a report in the MIB's database. To merit a report, you must have a serious medical condition or another factor that might affect your longevity, such as a poor driving record or an affinity for a dangerous sport like skydiving. The insurer decides whether to file a report on you with the MIB and, if so, what should be in it. The insurer may base its decision on information in your application, a physical examination, information from your doctor, or the insurer's own investigation of you.

Should you someday apply for another insurance policy, the new insurance company can request your report from the MIB and use it to learn about your history. The bureau says that it deletes information in a report after seven years.

Privacy advocates and consumers have long expressed concern about MIB reports and how they are used. According to the bureau's rules, an insurance company is not allowed either to turn an applicant down or to "rate" the applicant—charge a higher premium—solely on the basis of an MIB report. According to MIB President Neil Day, such practices violate the law in some states and make no sense because "companies are in the business of selling insurance, not denying it." Day also notes that some descriptions in bureau reports are sufficiently vague that they encourage an insurer to perform its own, more detailed, investigation.

According to Day, the MIB regularly audits insurers to ensure compliance with its rules, and it has the authority to suspend or fine a company that routinely violates them. Based on the results of those audits he concludes that violations are "very, very infrequent."

But Robert Ellis Smith, publisher of the newsletter *Privacy Journal* believes Day's estimate of the number of violations is way too low. Smith doesn't doubt that the bureau audits member companies, but he questions its practice of keeping audit results to itself, a serious issue for an organization in the touchy position of auditing the very companies that pay its expenses and sit on its board of directors. (Despite Day's assertion that MIB can punish violators, we found no example of a case in which action was taken.)

Smith also questions the state laws that Day says give consumers redress if an insurer rejects them based on an MIB report. Those laws are based on model legislation, known as the National Association of Insurance Commissioners Model Privacy Act, which was developed in the late 1970s with a good deal of input from the insurance industry. Smith who says he was the only consumer representative on the committee that drafted the model act, recalls the process as "a total farce. MIB was permitted to add amendments to that draft that pleased it."

"One critic of the MIB...has suggested MIB's error rate is much higher than 4 percent..."

Half a Million Errors?

Then there's the question of MIB's accuracy. Since even Day admits that 3 to 4 percent of MIB's database—or about half a million reports—is erroneous, insurance underwriters making decisions based solely on MIB reports could wrongly reject or overcharge many thousands of consumers every year. One critic of the MIB, Josh Kratka of the Massachusetts Public Interest Research Group, has suggested MIB's error rate is much higher than 4 percent, based on the rate of errors that exist in medical records themselves.

When the bureau has an erroneous report on you, things can get unpleasant. We spoke with two consumers who claimed that insurers turned them down based on their MIB reports. One, a California doctor, said her MIB report falsely said she suffered from Alzheimer's disease and had had a heart attack. The other, a West Coast man, said he found an erroneous diagnosis of drug and alcohol abuse in his reports.

Both people were put in the unenviable position of having to prove that they did not suffer from those conditions. Since MIB would take no responsibility for the content of its reports, both consumers had to figure out how to get insurance companies to correct the error, a time-consuming, trying process. "Why is the burden of proof on me, and why is that burden so great?" the West Coast man asked.

The Patient as Plaintiff

The MIB's Day says that consumers can take legal action if they can establish that insurers overcharged them or turned them down solely on the basis of an MIB report. That would be reassuring if an ordinary person stood much of a chance of getting the needed evidence. But a scofflaw insurer would be unlikely to admit to breaking MIB's rules. And an insurer may "explain" its decision simply by telling the applicant what medical condition the decision was based on, not where the information came from.

The MIB's home state of Massachusetts has passed what is probably the strongest law in the country relating to the bureau's work. Since 1992, insurance companies in that state have been required by law (rather than merely by MIB rules) to reinvestigate medical information disputed by an applicant. An applicant who disagrees with the results of that investigation can then appeal to the state insurance commissioner. In other states, the final decision still rests with the insurance company.

How secure MIB's system is remains uncertain. Bureau literature states that, to the organization's knowledge, no unauthorized person has ever gained access to the system. But a well-known private investigator in New York told our reporter that he could obtain an MIB report for us without sending a formal request to the bureau; he said that it had been done before.

What You Can Do

Before you apply for personal insurance, or if you have been rejected or "rated," request a report from the MIB at P.O. Box 105, Essex Station, Boston, Mass. 02112. Or call 617 4263660. There is no charge. If there is a report on you, it will typically arrive about a month after you send in MIB's request form. If the report contains errors, notify the bureau; it will tell you how to make a correction.

If you question an insurance company's decision, ask the company for a written description of the basis for that decision, including where it got its medical information.

When you fill out an insurance application, read the statement that authorizes the release of your medical information. If it seems too broad, modify it and initial the change. Insert changes that set some limits on the type of information that can be collected, as well as the time period and purpose for which it may be used. Some consumers have been successful using this tactic; others have not.

The $65-billion-a-year prescription-drug business has become so intensely competitive that manufacturers are resorting to extraordinary measures to get the edge. For example, drug makers now spend hundreds of millions of dollars to advertise prescription drugs directly to consumers in the hope they will ask their doctors for a prescription. This summer, the pharmaceutical company Miles Inc. agreed to pay 11 states a total of $605,000 to drop charges that it gave pharmacists $35 for each patient they switched to its hypertension drug from a competing brand.

Major drugmakers, such as Merck, SmithKline Beecham, and

Eli Lilly, are engineering corporate takeovers of companies that distribute drugs to consumers, primarily companies that administer company prescription benefit plans and those that sell prescription drugs by mail. Eli Lilly's recently proposed acquisition of PCS Health Systems, for example, would give the pharmaceutical company direct access to 50 million patients.

Every Other Prescription

To support their marketing programs, drugmakers also solicit patient lists from physicians and pharmacists. It has been estimated that information on nearly half of all U.S. prescriptions makes its way into one database or another.

Drugmakers also compile huge mailing lists through package inserts, mailings, and magazine and television ads that offer information about medications to people who call or write. A few years ago, half a million viewers in 16 states called a toll-free number on a TV commercial to find out the pollen count in their zip-code area. As a result of their inquiries, many callers received sales pitches for allergy medicine from Warner Lambert, the ad's sponsor. Using a similar approach, Johnson & Johnson compiled a list of 4.5 million women with incontinence who responded to an ad for its Serenity undergarments. A company spokesperson told us Johnson & Johnson has since taken the list off the market in response to privacy concerns.

At least one major mailing-list broker is making a name for itself in the corporate world by gathering the names of the ill. The firm, Metromail Corp., is a division of R.R. Donnelly & Sons, the giant magazine and catalog printer.

Metromail's best-known product is its National Consumer Data Base, which profiles about 92 million American households and 140 million individuals, including such information as product purchases and magazine subscriptions. Many organizations, including Consumers Union, the publisher of *Consumer Reports*, use Metromail's database to identify people who might be interested in their products. *Consumer Reports* does not supply information on its readers to Metromail.

Recently, Metromail has branched into the lucrative medical-database market with Patient Select, a million-name list of patients that it markets to the pharmaceutical industry. For about 30 cents per name, drugmakers like Marion Merrell Dow and Sandoz can pitch their wares directly to 3.5 million arthritics, a million diabetics, or 200,000 angina sufferers. The database includes a variety of other groups, such as sufferers of Alzheimer's or Parkinson's disease. (By policy, the names of cancer and AIDS patients are not collected.)

The company denies that Patient Select violates anyone's privacy because the names and health information are given voluntarily in response to ads and questionnaires. Metromail also discounts the danger that an insurance company may rent the list and then use the contents to deny anyone coverage. The company insists it wouldn't rent the list to an insurance company unless it determined the planned use was proper. But the standards of propriety applied to Patient Select remain entirely in the hands of Metromail.

What You Can Do

If you answer an ad for anything health-related, ask how the information being requested will be used.

If you aren't satisfied with the answer, think twice before giving your name or any other personal information.

If you do go ahead, give companies the minimum information they need. Your age and phone number are hardly necessary for a company to send you a brochure.

Fast-rising medical costs have given employers a greater interest in their employees' medical care and health status. Companies can save costs by helping employees stay healthy with wellness programs and exercise facilities. But employers can also cut costs in ways less appealing to employees, such as by making workers who smoke pay higher insurance premiums. They can even factor medical data into personnel decisions such as hiring, firing, and promotions.

Employers don't have a totally free hand to discriminate against workers based on their health. Federal law prohibits employers with more than 25 employees from requiring any medical information on an applicant before hiring. An employer also cannot require medical tests for an employee unless all employees with similar jobs are tested.

"...a University of Illinois study of Fortune 500 corporations found that fully half of the companies surveyed used employee medical records in making employment-related decisions."

Your Health, Your Career

But the rules don't run very deep. A few years back, a University of Illinois study of Fortune 500 corporations found that fully half of the companies surveyed used employee medical records in making employment-related decisions. And of those, nearly 20 percent didn't inform the employee. A 1991 survey by the Congressional Office of Technology Assessment found that almost a third of the employers that maintained employee medical records let their personnel departments read those records without notifying the employee.

Besides maintaining its own medical files, an employer may obtain medical information from the insurance carrier for the company's group health plan. Employers need some general information for legitimate purposes, such as monitoring the insurer's performance. Carriers we spoke with said they generally withheld identifiable records from employers. But the same protection doesn't hold for employees of companies that self-insure, a common practice among larger corporations.

When Companies Self-insure

Employees of self-insured companies may not even be aware of the practice, since their reimbursement checks may bear the name of an insurance company hired to process their claims but not to provide insurance. In the absence of an outside insurer, the employer owns the records relating to its employees' insurance claims. The companies that process claims for employers are, for the most part, bound to release employee data to them.

Some companies that serve self-insured clients told us that they do give employers identifiable information on employees, but with certain restrictions. Blue Cross of Nebraska will provide the information only on written request, only to certain employees at the company, and only for legitimate purposes. Capital Care of the District of Columbia alters records so the patient's name and Social Security number can't be identified, though it may still be possible to deduce an employee's identity from other information in some cases. Capital Care asks self-insured customers to indemnify it against employee lawsuits. Aetna requires a self-insured employer to state, in writing, what it will use the employee's medical information for; the use must be related to the insurance plan.

Despite such precautions, nothing can stop an unscrupulous employer from using employee information for purposes other than what it told its claims processor. According to Aetna, one client bluntly requested identifiable medical information so it could fire any employee who had AIDS. Even if the information doesn't lead to the employee's dismissal, it can prove embarrassing. A representative of San Francisco's Human Rights Commission told us that not a month goes by that she doesn't hear from employees who have received markedly different treatment from their fellow employees—discrimination, sympathy, or both—soon after they first used the company's health insurance for a serious illness such as AIDS.

There have also been press reports that some employers obtain medical information from company sponsored employee assistance programs—services that offer employees counseling or health advice. They then use that information to fight claims against the company or to shift medical costs to higher risk employees by charging them larger premiums.

The Employees Assistance Professionals Association, whose members administer such programs, insists that its members maintain confidentiality. Most of the information an assistance program releases, it says, is authorized by the employee, often in the course of filing a workers' compensation claim. The association's written standards require confidentiality except under special circumstances, such as court order or a law requiring disclosure. Whether those rules are sufficient to stop a scofflaw employer is another question.

What You Can Do

Find out your company's policies regarding the privacy of employee medical records. If you don't already know whether your company self-insures, ask.

If you plan to use an employee assistance program, ask the provider under what circumstances information about you could be given to your employer. Before you sign a release, make sure it sets clear limits on the type of personal information that will be collected.

Who's Looking at Your Files?[4]

U.S. Representative Nydia Velazquez, 43, knows how easy it is for medical secrets to find their way out of a doctor's files. When Velazquez was running for Congress in 1992 to represent New York City's 12th Congressional District, someone got hold of hospital records detailing her 1991 suicide attempt and forwarded them by anonymous fax to the press. The New York Post broke the story, and Velazquez was forced to acknowledge publicly something even her family did not know: she had tried to kill herself with sleeping pills and vodka. Despite the painful publicity, she won the election—and now she is suing the hospital for $10 million.

Public figures are not the only ones who should be worried about the confidentiality of their medical records. Last month a coalition of groups that help AIDS patients in Boston went to court in an effort to stop auditors at the Department of Health and Human Services from passing on the names of patients in various AIDS programs to other government agencies. And two weeks ago two Marines were court-martialed for refusing to provide the military with samples of their DNA, something the Pentagon now demands of all service personnel.

> *"Companies and government agencies have already claimed the right to tap individual health files."*

The Marines' fear was that the information would wind up in the hands of a future employer or insurer. That fear was well placed. Companies and government agencies have already claimed the right to tap individual health files. More than a quarter of Americans responding to a 1993 Harris poll said health information about them had been improperly disclosed. The issue has caught Congress's attention: legislation designed to protect medical-record privacy—but which critics say is too lax—is pending before the Senate.

Medical records contain some of the most sensitive of personal information—including sexual orientation, past drug use and genetic predisposition to various diseases. As part of the Hippocratic oath, physicians promise to keep whatever they learn about a patient to themselves. But it's hard to keep a secret if more than a couple of people are in on it; in a typical five-day stay at a teaching hospital, as many as 150 people—from nursing staff to X-ray technicians to billing clerks—have legitimate access to a single patient's records.

Now hospitals are rushing to computerize those records, raising the fear that medical secrets could be accessed, copied and distributed with a few clicks of a mouse. There are plenty of good reasons to gather such information: to spot previously unknown drug interactions, for example, or to provide early warning of a

---

4 Article by Christine Gorman, from *Time* 147:60-2 My 6, '96. Copyright © 1996 Time Inc. Reprinted with permission.

newly emerging epidemic. But once the records have been digitized, they can be transmitted without a trace all over the globe.

Some hospitals are even talking about storing patient files on the World Wide Web—albeit behind so-called fire walls that use passwords to separate a hospital's "intranet" from the Internet. But passwords are notoriously easy to guess or steal, and fire walls have been breached by hackers who have no motivation other than to see what's on the other side. Others may have strong economic incentives for trolling the medical-record data stream. Pharmaceutical firms building direct-mail advertising lists for a new drug will pay top dollar for the names and addresses of people taking competing medications. And life-insurance companies could save lots of money if they knew in advance which of their applicants were likely to get sick and die.

"Pharmaceutical firms building direct-mail advertising lists for a new drug will pay top dollar for the names...."

Often the data traded in what has become a $40 billion health-information industry are provided by the patients themselves, who commonly give blanket access to their medical records when they sign insurance waivers. Sometimes, however, the data collection isn't quite so aboveboard. In 1993 a health-care newsletter reported that a banker serving on a state health commission had pulled up a list of everyone who was battling cancer in his area. The banker then checked it against a list of customers at his bank and called in the loans of the cancer patients. In another case, a dozen Medicaid clerks in Maryland sold (for as little as 50¢ a record) individual profiles from the state's computerized database to HMO recruiters. The recruiters used the information to target potential customers and sometimes even enrolled customers without their knowledge or consent.

Although the Medicaid clerks were caught and fined, the banker's name was never made public and he was never punished. Patients have little legal recourse. Sixteen states in the U.S. provide no explicit guarantees for medical-record privacy, and the others vary widely in the kinds of disclosure they allow and whether or not patient consent is required.

Last fall two Senators, Republican Robert Bennett of Utah and Democrat Patrick Leahy of Vermont, introduced a bill that would provide a uniform standard for protecting medical records. Much to the Senators' surprise, their bill was quickly attacked by some privacy advocates for setting the bar too low. "The devil is in the details," says Dr. Denise Nagel, head of the Coalition for Patient Rights of New England. "As it's currently written, this bill allows greater, not lesser, access to medical records." Even doctors' groups have expressed concern; in February the American Medical Association announced its opposition to the current Bennett-Leahy measure. The bill is being reworked and may reach the full Senate later this spring.

At the heart of the controversy is the issue of just how much privacy is enough. According to a TIME/CNN poll, most Americans (87% of respondents) believe patients should be asked for permission every time any information about them is used. But some experts, like Lawrence Gostin of Georgetown University Law Center, regard that view as outdated. "I know what I'm suggesting will not perfectly protect privacy," he says, "[but] the widespread collection of health information has enormous benefits for the American public."

One of those benefits could be a national health database. In such a system, detailed information about all 250 million Americans would be available electronically. That way, if a cross-country traveler was knocked unconscious in a car accident, doctors could punch up his or her medical records to determine the best treatment. With such a system, public-health officials could keep better track of epidemics, for example, or the emergence of a drug-resistant strain of tuberculosis. Researchers could scan the population to identify important risk factors that increase a woman's chances of developing breast cancer. AT&T is helping create such a network of linked records for the National Health Service of Britain. Doctors there, however, have strongly opposed the system at every turn. "We don't believe it's prudent to put personal health information on millions of people in the same place," says Ross Anderson, a lecturer at Cambridge University. "It creates too big a target."

A recent investigation by the *Sunday Times* of London found that for a fee of as little as $225, British detective agencies routinely obtain medical records simply by phoning doctors' receptionists and pretending to be another doctor's secretary. Today a few thousand records may get tapped that way. The fear is that the proposed National Health Service network would multiply the problem. "If the receptionists of all Britain's 32,000 general practitioners have their systems linked up so that any of them can access all the information," says Anderson, "then you've had it. We will do whatever is in our power to make sure that this does not come to pass."

There are ways to make electronic records more secure, but those measures can be expensive, and they must be built into a system at the beginning. At Boston's Beth Israel Hospital, an electronic audit trail keeps track of everyone who accesses the computerized records, and doctors have the option of tagging certain records as particularly sensitive—triggering an alert whenever a request is made to see that information. Even so, the hospital found that once the system was in place, it was impractical to declare any area of the electronic record completely off-limits.

In an effort to stem the unchecked flow of information, some doctors have started censoring themselves. "These days, insurance companies don't want summaries; they want the whole record," says Dr. Nancy Dickey, chairman of the board of trustees of the American Medical Association. "So I think twice about what I include. Then I hope I can remember it all." She is worried that too much data sharing will jeopardize the doctor-patient relationship: "If my patients fear that what they tell me could

"The fear is that the proposed National Health Service network would multiply the problem."

come back to haunt them, they'll tend to be less forthright. I may come up with the wrong treatment because I was chasing the wrong clues."

The threat to confidentiality will only grow as genetic testing becomes more common. Once doctors learn about potential dangers lurking in their patients' DNA—diseases they don't have but may be at risk of contracting—few will be able to claim a clean bill of health. That is what prompted Corporals John Mayfield of Dallas and Joseph Vlacovsky of Canton, Ohio, to refuse the military's demand for a sample of their DNA. (The Pentagon wants its personnel's DNA on file in case it might ever need help in identifying their remains.) The men faced six months in the stockade and dishonorable discharges. But the military judge apparently found some merit in their concerns; he ruled that they were only to be confined to base for seven days. And that they could keep their DNA.

The soldiers' genetic data are safe for now. Whether their secrets—and those of hundreds of millions of civilians—will be kept tomorrow may depend on the safeguards being proposed today.

Censoring the Right to Live[5]

The First Amendment is usually thought of as protecting freedom of expression, but there's another dimension of its scope—the freedom to receive expression, including information.

In constitutional law, the clearest statement of that freedom is in the 1982 Supreme Court decision *Board of Education, Island Trees Union Free School District v. Pico*. It was a public-school-censorship case, and Justice William Brennan made the point—an obvious one, but one little noted in Court chronicles—that there is indeed a right "to receive information and ideas." That right "follows ineluctably from the sender's right to send [information].... More importantly, the right to receive ideas is a necessary predicate to the recipient's meaningful exercise of his own rights of speech, press, and political freedom."

In forty-four states, the freedom to receive information is being lethally violated. And those responsible for this censoring of information that would prevent deaths are not Jesse Helms or the Christian Right. In New York, the only state where there is a public debate on this issue, the censors of life—with some internal dissenters—are gays, abortion-rights forces, and, most grotesquely, the American Civil Liberties Union.

The public battle began with Nettie Mayersohn, a member of the New York State Assembly. She is so forceful a feminist that in 1989, the state's chapter of the National Organization for Women acclaimed her as the feminist legislator of the year. But now, Mayersohn is a pariah among many feminists who support abortion rights, even though she is still firmly pro-choice.

She became a heretic when she introduced a bill in the Assembly that would make a basic change in the testing of newborns in New York. In New York, as in forty-three other states, all babies are tested to find out whether they have syphilis, hepatitis, sickle-cell anemia, and other medical conditions needing quick attention. The infants are also tested for HIV infection. But the HIV results are not given to the mother or to the physician.

As Nettie Mayersohn makes clear, "Seventy-five percent of the newborns who are HIV-positive at birth turn out not to be HIV cases. They have the mother's antibodies, which their own bodies throw off." The other 25 percent, however, actually are HIV-positive. In New York State, that means a quarter of the 1,512 infants found positive in the blind test do have the virus that leads to AIDS.

Mayersohn's bill would have ensured mandatory identification of HIV infants—mothers and their doctors would be told of their

---

[5] Article by Nat Hentoff, author of *Free Speech for Me–But Not for Thee*, from *The Progressive* 59:19-20 F '95. Copyright © 1995 Nat Hentoff. Reprinted with permission.

babies' condition, and the health department would be required
to see that all such infants were treated.

Why, then, was her bill so fiercely opposed—with considerable
money spent lobbying against it—by such liberal groups as NOW,
NARAL, gays, and that paladin of free expression, the ACLU?

Disclosing that an infant has the HIV virus means that the
mother is infected and has been tested without her consent. As
a result, say the opponents of disclosure, the mother becomes
vulnerable to discrimination and stigmatization. The mother's
privacy in this context, say Mayersohn's opponents, must take
precedence over the infant's life.

The coldness of this approach is shown in a corollary contentious issue. In November, *CBS Evening News* did a report on
the discovery that AZT, taken during pregnancy, could prevent
many infants being born with the HIV virus. Dr. Philip Pizzo of
the National Institutes of Health suggested that many children's
lives could be saved if all pregnant women were tested for AIDS
and offered the AZT.

Speaking for the opposition was Dr. Ruth Macklin, a bioethicist
at the Albert Einstein College of Medicine in New York. "It is an
invasion of privacy. It threatens the women's interests."

Asked "Is freedom that important that you might allow 15,000
babies' lives to be poured down the drain?" Macklin replied, "At
a certain point, one balances freedom against lives, indeed. We
fight wars to preserve our freedom, knowing that a certain number of people are going to die."

It has been said—by me, anyway—that many bioethicists have
formed a new priesthood of death.

As for Nettie Mayersohn and her continuing fight to save lives
in this war, she says, "Countless people tell me that I will be
destroying the mother's privacy and also that she has the right
not to know. They completely dismiss the fact that there is now
another human life involved whose right to medical care—and
indeed to life—is being violated. It's a baby, not a statistic!

"Look, the New York State Health Department and the Federal
Centers for Disease Control recommend that if a woman knows
she is HIV-infected, she should be warned not to breast-feed her
child." But these mothers are being sent home from the hospital
without being told they're infected.

The child, then, is likely to be hit, within months, with devas-
tating attacks of opportunistic infections thriving on a weakened
immune system.

What of the mother's right not to know? She can't evade knowing her child's HIV status because, as a number of physicians
who treat youngsters with AIDS have emphasized, "Sooner or
later, HIV will declare itself. The goal of newborn testing is to
identify infection before it is too late to prevent certain consequences."

A persistent argument against mandatory identification of HIV
infants is that the mother, if she discovers she is infected, will

> *"Disclosing that an infant has the HIV virus means that the mother is infected and has been tested without her consent."*

panic and flee the health-care system. I've heard this from gays, abortion rights activists, and leading officials of the ACLU.

None of these opponents of disclosing the HIV results has given a single example of a mother who found out, after taking her baby home, that she and her child were HIV-infected—and then disappeared in panic.

And I have told them that they have a patronizing attitude toward the many black and Latino women in this situation. The stereotype is that these women do not care as much about their children as do whites and, accordingly, would remove them from health care. Jim Dwyer of *Newsday* has interviewed a number of black and Latino women who are furious "that they were never told that they and their infants were at grave risk."

Said one woman whose son has become very sick: "I should have known so I could take care of myself—and him."

These women do not have any political clout. The awful surprises experienced by them and their children are permitted, as Dwyer writes in his column, because "the black and Latino kids who die of this disease don't have the political power or money to spend on lobbyists to compete with NOW or the Gay Men's Health Crisis."

The lobbyists against Mayersohn urge that there be mandatory counseling instead of mandatory HIV testing. With counseling, it is said, new mothers will eventually be persuaded to be tested for HIV. The problem is that counseling has largely failed. First of all, a considerable number of the pregnant women at issue don't show up at a hospital until it's time to give birth. So they can't be counseled beforehand. Others who are in the health system are often very reluctant to be persuaded by counseling.

Accordingly, says Dr. Keith Krasinski at Bellevue—who works with HIV-infected children—"Every child must be identified for HIV at birth, so that he or she can be treated. To do less is discrimination in its cruelest form."

The forces against unblinding this information often cite Harlem Hospital in New York City as a resplendent illustration that the voluntary approach—counseling—can work.

Yet Dr. Elaine Abrams, director of Pediatric AIDS Care—including the voluntary counseling program—at Harlem Hospital, emphasizes, "I'd like to see HIV testing as routine as syphilis testing or eye drops at birth. Let's treat this as a disease—not a political problem."

A majority of the physicians on New York's Committee for the Care of Children and Adolescents with HIV Infection agree with Dr. Abrams. This is the one committee in the state with direct, long-term experience treating and caring for precisely the children this debate is about. The physicians in the majority point out that HIV-specialized medical care and other interventions "improve the outcome of HIV-infected children, resulting in better and longer life.... The potential benefits to HIV-infected children, identified at birth, are sufficient to support the 'doctrine of

parental override' whereby the potential benefit to the infant outweighs the mother's right to refuse consent for HIV testing."

Mayersohn's bill was killed by the State Assembly leadership in
the 1994 session—with Governor Mario Cuomo cravenly staying
out of the debate, although he acknowledged to Jim Dwyer of
Newsday that the life of a child is more vital than even privacy.
After all, these are not fetuses. Newborn children have the due-
process and equal-protection-of-the-laws rights that all persons
have under the Constitution.

Mayersohn, however, has by no means given up. Before the
Assembly adjourned, she went to the floor of that institution and
spoke of "powerful groups who have a determination that they
own [AIDS]—and there can be no changes in health law without
their approval. As a result we will continue to send thousands of
newborns home from the hospital to suffer the miseries of pre-
ventable opportunistic infections—and a premature death....

"Last week, with great fanfare and a slap on the back for ourselves, we passed a much-needed domestic-violence law. I submit to you that our failure to pass a mandatory testing bill makes
us accomplices in the cruelest and most obscene violence—the
abuse and neglect of the most neglected children in our state....

"We protect newborn infants from a whole host of diseases by
doing mandatory testing. This is considered enlightened public-
health policy.... Why do we not do the same for babies with
AIDS? It is because the religious Left has declared that there is
something different about the disease, and if babies have to be
sacrificed on the altar of confidentiality, so be it....

"This issue will not be laid to rest here today.... There are people who care enough to keep it alive. Child advocates, reporters,
doctors, mothers, and the hundreds of thousands of citizens
across the country who are astounded by what we are doing here
in Albany by ignoring that these babies are independent, living,
breathing human beings whose right to health care is being violated."

Meanwhile, a dissident chapter of the state affiliate of the
National Organization for Women—in Ulster County—supports
Nettie Mayersohn and her bill, noting that "NOW should be leading the fight on this public issue. If the well-being of women and
their children is not the concern of NOW, who will speak for
them?"

There is now a Republican governor of New York State, George
Pataki, who, while in the State Senate, supported the Mayersohn
bill. Unfortunately, Assembly Speaker Sheldon Silver, now the most
powerful Democrat in the state, was the man who killed the bill last
term by offering a weak alternative that impressed hardly anyone.
But the battle will also be pursued in the courts—on the grounds
of equal protection of the laws (the Fourteenth Amendment), and
provisions in the Americans with Disabilities Act.

Meanwhile, infants are dying because their parents have had
their First Amendment right—to receive information—denied.

Shoring Up Protection of
Personal Health Data[6]

Few Americans are likely to see their private medical information become a newspaper headline as the late tennis great Arthur Ashe did when it was revealed without his permission that he had AIDS. But we all have reason to be concerned about the confidentiality and accuracy of our personal health data.

Medical records of average citizens have been posted in a computerized record system without adequate safeguards in Massachusetts, dumped in a parking lot after the closing of a psychiatric clinic in Louisiana, and sold in Maryland. At least one company that legally buys medical records from a variety of organizations has reported that the records often include patient names (which it says it removes before selling the data to drug companies). In several instances, employers have received information from insurers that allowed them to determine that employees had AIDS or received psychiatric treatment. Moreover, errors in medical records are difficult to correct. A computer error at the Medical Information Bureau, a Boston-based consortium of health, life, and disability insurers that maintains a database on 15 million Americans, resulted in one patient being denied health insurance for 18 months. The error was not corrected until the state insurance commissioner intervened.

"A computer error at the Medical Information Bureau...that maintains a database on 15 million Americans, resulted in one patient being denied health insurance for 18 months."

Congress is now considering legislation that would, for the first time, provide federal legal protection for personal health data collected by organizations outside the federal government. Although early prospects were promising—the legislation had powerful bipartisan sponsorship and support—passage is now uncertain. Policymakers who were focused on specific personal health data issues unexpectedly became enmeshed in the broader, long-standing debate about balancing individual rights with community needs. The central question changed from "How should our nation deal with personal health data as a matter of law?" to "How do we define privacy in contemporary society?" This shift in focus threatens to derail what may be our best opportunity to implement a much-needed federal policy for protecting personal health data.

Benefits of Confidentiality

Since the days of Hippocrates, the medical profession has dedicated itself to protecting patient information. Physician commit-

6 Article by Don E. Detmer, University Professor of Health Policy and Surgery and senior vice president at the University of Virginia, Charlottesville, also chairs the Institute of Medicine's Board on Health Care Services and Elaine B. Steen, assistant to the senior vice president at the University of Virginia, from *Issues in Science and Technology* 12:73-8 Sum '96. Copyright © 1996 *Issues in Science and Technology*. Reprinted with permission.

ment to confidentiality enables a patient to share sensitive personal information and increases the likelihood that the physician will have complete data on which to base clinical judgments. This improves the chances for accurate diagnosis and better clinical outcomes. At a more fundamental level, some patients will not even seek care unless they believe that a health care professional or organization will maintain confidentiality. Individuals seeking mental health services, for example, are legitimately concerned that errant information going to employers or others could come back to harm them.

Many Americans are unaware that U.S. citizens do not necessarily have legal recourse if they are harmed by inappropriate disclosure of their medical records. Legal protection for personal health data depends in large measure on the state in which the data reside. In some states, movie rental records are better protected than medical records. Nor do all U.S. citizens have the right to view their medical records and correct inaccuracies.

"Legal protection for personal health data depends in large measure on the state...."

This uneven and unsettling situation has arisen because legal protection for confidentiality of personal health data derives from a complicated combination of federal and state statutes, regulations, and common law, rather than from a sound and consistent policy framework. Inequities aside, the logistics of the situation are becoming increasingly unmanageable. Due to the growing mobility of the U.S. population, an individual's health-related records are commonly scattered among several states. Differences in state laws can lead to jurisdictional nightmares, creating unnecessary confusion and costs and impeding the timely transfer of information needed for patient care.

Concerns about adequate protection of personal information are not new, nor are they limited to health care. In 1974, Congress passed the Federal Privacy Act, which established the right of citizens to know that certain personal information is available in a record system as well as the purpose of that information. The act also established the right to access the information, have a copy made, and correct or amend the records. Furthermore, the act stipulated that the information may not be used for any purpose beyond that for which it was collected and may not be disclosed to any person or organization without the consent of the subject of the records. Disclosure is, however, permitted without consent for certain routine uses such as civil and criminal law enforcement and scientific research using nonidentifiable information.

The privacy act applies to all federal agencies, including health care facilities operated by the federal government. There is, however, no federal law protecting the confidentiality of health information collected by other organizations. In 1985, the National Conference of Commissioners on Uniform State Laws, an organization supported by the states, developed model legislation to stimulate consistency among states on health care information management issues. But more than a decade later, only two states have enacted the model legislation.

Why Action Is Needed

A combination of forces has heightened the need for federal action. First, the ever-increasing capabilities of medicine, combined with the aging of the population, have resulted in more data being collected. Soon our records will contain not only information on diseases that we have already experienced, but on diseases that we might experience in the future. Second, the increasing complexity of health care delivery has increased the number of legitimate users and uses of patient information. Third, as health care delivery systems are increasingly integrated, organizations with large databases will come to control access to our data. Finally, advances in information and communications technology make it possible to store more data online at lower cost, transfer data electronically, and link independent episodes of care to form a single patient record.

Each of these developments increases the opportunities for willful misuse of personal health data, which must be offset by technological safeguards such as encryption and audit trails as well as institutional policies, educational programs, and procedures. Federal policy, particularly sanctions for breaches of confidentiality, would significantly strengthen existing measures by putting all data handlers on notice that they are responsible for protecting these records.

Just before the health care reform debate of the early 1990s, the Institute of Medicine (IOM) released a report calling computer-based patient records (CPRs) an essential technology for health care. This report proved prescient not only in defining a vision for CPRs but also in describing the information management capabilities and information infrastructure that health care will need to transform itself in the coming decade. The vision for robust CPRs was consistent with the health care delivery system outlined in the Clinton administration's failed health care reform proposal; it is equally relevant for its replacement, a market-driven revolution in health care delivery.

If the United States is to develop an accessible, effective, and affordable health care system, health care professionals will need to have access to all clinically relevant information as well as support in the form of alerts and reminders. In other words, CPR systems must be widely available and routinely used. Equally important, use of CPRs would also strengthen the scientific base for medicine by making it easier to develop aggregated clinical databases for research and to collect measurements of psychosocial dimensions of illness and treatment (such as patient satisfaction and impacts on health status and function) in addition to traditional physiologic and metabolic measurements.

The ultimate success of CPRs depends on and drives the need for sound policies to protect patient data. The IOM patient record study committee identified the lack of clear policies to protect

"...use of CPRs would also strengthen the scientific base for medicine by making it easier to develop aggregated clinical databases...."

confidentiality as a barrier—adding costs and time—to the development and implementation of CPRs. If physicians and patients do not believe that the information CPRs contain is protected, they will not be used to their full advantage. Given the inevitable diffusion of CPRs throughout the health care system, policy must keep up with—and if possible stay ahead of—technology. Other information technologies raise similar issues. Telemedicine promises patients and doctors in isolated regions access to state-of-the-art care but can only attain that goal if it is based on accurate data and the confidence of patients and health care professionals.

The call for federal action has become increasingly specific. A 1995 IOM report, Health Data in the Information Age, examined the potential that health database organizations offer for improving health and the performance of the health care system. The report recommended that Congress enact preemptive legislation that "will establish a uniform requirement for the assurance of confidentiality and protection of privacy rights for person-identifiable health data." In 1993, the Office of Technology Assessment (OTA) found that current laws do not provide consistent comprehensive protection of health information. In its 1995 report, Bringing Health Care Online: The Role of Information Technologies, OTA noted the need for federal legislation and regulation to protect the confidentiality of medical information.

After the demise of the Clinton administration's health care plan, several bills were introduced during the 103rd Congress that proposed incremental changes in health care policy. Among these were several health information privacy bills. Although a wide range of organizations and groups, including the American Medical Association, testified in support, no measure was enacted. In 1995, a coalition of individuals and organizations drafted a confidentiality bill designed to build on the consensus achieved during the previous session of Congress. The result, the Medical Records Confidentiality Act (S. 1360), was introduced in October 1995, sponsored by Senators Robert Bennett (R-Utah), Bob Dole (R-Kan.), Nancy Kassebaum (R-Kan.), Edward Kennedy (D-Mass.), and Patrick Leahy (D-Vt.), among others. Two other bills are also being considered: H.R. 435, introduced by Rep. Gary Condit (D.-Calif.), and H.R. 3482, introduced by Rep. Jim McDermott (D.-Wash.).

Senate Bill Stands Out

Of these bills, we believe that the Bennett bill (S. 1360) provides the most balanced approach to a sound policy framework for protecting personal health data. It focuses specifically and deliberately on confidentiality rather than privacy; seeks to keep third parties who are not in a confidential relationship with the subject of a record from having access without the subject's consent; ensures that every citizen has access to and can get copies of personal health information except where disclosure could endanger someone; defines protected health information as well as the roles of those who come into contact with others' health data; requires health information trustees to establish appropriate safeguards "to ensure the confidentiality, security, accuracy, and integrity of personal health information"; and creates an advisory committee to the secretary of the Department of Health and Human Services to ensure sensible policy development over time. Above all, it limits the use of personal health data to the purposes for which it was collected and establishes sanctions for knowingly obtaining or disclosing protected health information.

S. 1360 requires that the person who is the subject of protected health information authorize disclosure for treatment and payment either in writing or by electronic authentication. Health information trustees may disclose protected data to certified health information services in a form that cannot be traced back to any individual patient. Exceptions to the limited disclosure rule are quite specific. They include emergencies, authorized public health activities (disease or injury reports, surveillance, and investigations), health research authorized by a certified institutional review board, judicial proceedings, and law enforcement.

"S. 1360...gives patients greater and more explicit control over their personal health data...."

S. 1360 represents a huge stride toward strengthening the confidentiality of personal health data in the United States. By establishing a minimum standard of access and protection, it overcomes the disparities among state laws. It gives patients greater and more explicit control over their personal health data, limits the uses of that data, and puts individuals and institutions on notice that they will pay a price for willful, inappropriate disclosure. In establishing the advisory panel, the bill recognizes that solutions will need to be refined as technology and health care delivery continue to evolve. Moreover, it achieves these objectives without creating significant additional burdens and costs for the health care system.

Given the complexity of this issue, it is not surprising that response to the bill has been varied. Many groups—including the AIDS Action Council, the American Health Information Management Association, the Computer-based Patient Record Institute, and the Center for Democracy and Technology—hailed the bill as a positive response to the risk of misuse of personal health data. Organizations that provide health care services in more than one state are pleased by the potential for reducing their costs.

Some groups support the concept of the bill but have concerns about specific aspects of it. They question whether the proposed legislation would impose greater administrative burdens and hence greater financial and human costs on health care delivery organizations. Some seek stronger safeguards on the use of personal data for research and law enforcement.

Opponents of the bill include the Consumer Project on Technology (a Ralph Nader group), the Justice Resources

Institute (a Boston-based health advocacy group), and the Coalition for Patient Rights; some health care professionals who do not want to give patients access to their records; and people who interpret the absence of a direct prohibition on large data banks as an implicit desire for their creation. Finally, some people disparage the bill, arguing that it does not go far enough to protect patient privacy.

Communitarians Versus Individualists

This last controversy has not been resolved. Although both sides of the debate favor strengthening protections for personal health information, there are profound differences in how they view the control and use of such information and in how that view moves from the abstract to application in a real and increasingly computer-based world. Those supporting the current legislation might be described as communitarians. They believe that most physicians, hospitals, insurers, researchers, and public health workers are responsible about protecting patient information. They acknowledge that the rise of CPRs will increase the volume and movement of personal health data but believe that with appropriate safeguards CPRs can be more secure than paper-based records have been.

Proponents of this view hold that legislation to alert people handling personal health data that they have more than a moral responsibility for these data is in the public interest and that this could be accomplished without disruption of present practices except to improve procedures and performance. Furthermore, they believe that having access to personal health data for purposes of health services and other medical research as well as public health is of such compelling importance that they would allow access if certain conditions are met and procedures followed. They seem willing to trust one another with what may be sensitive personal information in the interests of rendering care under life-threatening conditions, as well as performing legitimate research, which has clearly demonstrated that it can improve human life.

On balance, this position is mostly concerned with confidentiality and less concerned with privacy. The communitarian position assumes that sufficient societal and personal goods will be derived from sharing collective experience and information accessible under circumscribed conditions to more than offset injuries that may occur from an invasion of personal privacy (which from time to time will happen regardless of what system is in place). In operational terms, the goal is to assure that personal health data are treated with great respect and regard and that breaches in such treatment are dealt with by graded sanctions.

The individualist viewpoint holds that privacy is a right of such overriding importance that access to personal health information should not be available for any use unless expressly permitted by the patient and his or her physician. As a principle, this is laudable. Operationally, it is impossible. Seeking approvals from patients and physicians for the myriad interactions that are part of our modern health care system would add even more to the paper blizzard physicians must deal with today. One of two possible outcomes would be likely to occur. The authorizations approved in the forms patients sign would be broadened to allow release of information for a wide range of potential uses simply to get around the complicated and costly (in time and money) business of tracking patients down later. Or, equally likely, approvals would be withheld or doctors would not even try to get them for purposes such as medical research and public health, simply to avoid hassles.

This approach is characteristic of a movement within the law in favor of individual choice. At its most extreme, proponents seek the power of law in order to serve individual tastes even if they are at the direct expense of the common good. Community needs or social connections may be important but are not compelling. This viewpoint holds that no common good outweighs individual freedoms.

"...proponents seek the power of law in order to serve individual tastes even if they are at the direct expense of the common good."

The Case for Confidentiality

There are two reasons why communitarians, such as ourselves, find it difficult to understand the reluctance of individualists to support S. 1360 as a fallback from their desire for much more stringent regulations. First, the proposed legislation would set a national standard of practice that is higher than any current state standard. Second, the current situation could deteriorate while debate about privacy goes endlessly on.

Communitarians also worry that mechanisms required to achieve the level of privacy sought by individualists would shut down the flow of information in health care and significantly effect the operation of the health care system. Individualists tend to discount the costs of managing personal health data under the restrictions they would impose. In an era when cost control is a powerful driver of change in the health care system, aggregated patient data are all the more important to measure quality of care, track accountability of health care providers, and establish the effectiveness of alternative interventions. If patients are allowed to prevent even nonidentifiable data from being added to research databases, sample sizes will quickly diminish to the point where statistically valid results cannot be achieved. In addition, if the cost of obtaining required authorizations becomes too high, levels of research are likely to decline. Public health activities are also at risk if aggregation of patient data becomes more difficult, as they rely heavily on assessment and surveillance to identify problems, provide data to assist decisionmakers, and monitor the progress of programs.

The individualists' concerns should not be ignored. We cannot afford to be complacent about privacy and confidentiality. The potential harm to citizens is real and can be substantial. Even though almost all aspects of our society, particularly health care, have come to depend on the flow of personal information, we should never accept anything less than unquestionable confidentiality of that information at all levels.

This commitment to confidentiality must begin with the individuals entrusted with the information, continue with the institutions that manage the information, and be buttressed by a federal policy framework that provides a coherent approach to managing personal health data in the information age. Moreover, rules of confidentiality must be complemented by rules of privacy, because individuals outside a confidential relationship who inappropriately obtain or disclose personal health data cannot be charged with violating confidentiality.

"A 1993 Harris-Equifax poll found that 80 percent of respondents were concerned about threats to the privacy of their health information."

If Congress turns to the public for guidance on this issue, it will find that Americans are of two minds about privacy. We want our privacy respected, yet we tolerate and sometimes support open and aggressive news media whose behavior has become increasingly intrusive. A 1993 Harris-Equifax poll found that 80 percent of respondents were concerned about threats to the privacy of their health information. Yet in West Virginia, some patients are allowing their physicians to put unencrypted data about their health on the Internet's World Wide Web to facilitate the sharing of records during consultations with other physicians and to make records accessible when patients arrive at hospitals. Patients involved in the project have indicated that the benefits outweigh the potential risks of privacy invasion. Thus, we believe that if forced to choose, more Americans would likely favor the blessings of good medical care and the potential for future cures through medical research over the hope of creating an airtight system for personal privacy in an open society.

The question, not only for Congress but for all citizens, is this: While the debate between communitarians and individualists over how to deal with personal health data continues, can we at least make progress toward confidentiality? If the current stalemate persists, we risk Congress adjourning without passing any law protecting medical information. The undesirable result would be a continued lack of consistent nationwide safeguards. If we miss this opportunity to improve the protection of medical records, we will have secured neither privacy nor confidentiality.

RECOMMENDED READING
Information about all the pending confidentiality legislation discussed here can be found at the following:
  World Wide Web sites:
  http://amia.org/lkpp.html
  http://rs9.loc.gov/

Predictive Genetic Testing: Ethical, Legal, and Social Implications[7]

Imagine visiting your physician for a routine physical, and he or she recommends that you have a new genetic test run on a small sample of your blood. The doctor informs you that it will indicate your chances for developing certain diseases at some point in the future, including breast and colon cancer, heart disease, diabetes, and Alzheimer's. The physician also assures you that you have no physical symptoms of any of these conditions and, even if the test indicates the likelihood of a disease, you may not have any symptoms for years, if ever. It is explained that, if the results indicate a probability of increased risk for one or more of these diseases, there are no preventive treatments. The doctor notes that you might be able to reduce the risk by lifestyle changes, such as controlled diet and smoking cessation. If the condition does manifest itself, some treatment options may be available, but they are limited and frequently invasive.

Although such a test might be a major advance for predicting future health risks and preventive medicine, it also would raise a host of complex social and ethical issues for the patient and physician. For example: Would the anxiety of living with the likelihood of one or more specific, chronic, debilitating diseases create psychological burdens that outweigh the therapeutic potential of lifestyle changes or earlier treatment due to increased vigilance? If no effective interventions are known, would it be better to live without knowing your genetic fate, or to understand the chances of disease in order to make life plans accordingly? Would you tell your spouse about the prospect of genetically influenced disease? Your fiancee? Would they have a right to know? Would it be unethical to have children to whom you might pass along the risk of the genetic susceptibility? Would you tell your employer or a prospective employer? Would you notify your insurance company? Would you apply for more life or health insurance? Would your employer and insurance company have a right to learn the test results and use them in employment and employee benefit decisions?

Predictive genetic tests are not merely science fiction; neither are they projections of a remote time in the future. A few already are in use, while others are in the development stage and will be available soon. These powerful new medical tools soon will help physicians make early predictions of potential chronic health

---

7 Article by Bill Allen and Ray Moseley, instructor and associate professor, respectively, medical Hemonities program, University of Florida College of Medicine, Gainseville, from *USA Today* 123:66-8 N '94. Copyright © 1994 *USA Today*. Reprinted with permission.

problems and, perhaps, allow early intervention. In order to minimize the quandaries that may accompany such advances, the social and ethical consequences of genetic information with predictive significance must be anticipated.

Begun in 1990 by the National Institutes of Health and the U.S. Department of Energy, the Human Genome Initiative (HGI) is a 15-year coordinated research endeavor. The goal is to locate and identify the functions of the 50,000-100,000 genes that determine human hereditary characteristics, with a special focus on those that affect health and longevity.

"The goal is to locate and identify the functions of the 50,000-100,000 genes that determine human hereditary characteristics...."

Even when a genetic "map" is complete and the sequence of human deoxyribonucleic acid (DNA) has been deciphered, it will take decades of additional research to understand the functions of genes more fully. Yet, the impact of what is discovered in the next dozen years likely will be useful enough to warrant expert projections that individuals will carry their own distinctive, complete genetic codes on the 21st-century equivalent of a compact disc. The U.S. military already is using such information as a more definitive means of identification than dog tags or dental records, and some hospitals have begun to use genetic identification of newborns to prevent the types of mix-ups at birth that resulted in the Kimberly Mays case.

Although the project is in its early stages, the medical and social impact of such genetic research is being felt. So far, most of the advances have focused on 4,000 identified disorders that require an abnormality in only one gene to cause the associated genetic disease. Considered individually, these single-gene ailments are rare, but collectively they affect approximately one percent of the population. HGI-sponsored researchers, however, are beginning to identify the role genes play in more common health disorders.

Genetic abnormalities are thought to be a significant factor in cardiovascular disease, certain types of cancers, diabetes, and neurodegenerative disorders such as Alzheimer's disease. The role played by genetic factors in these common diseases is more complex than in those directly caused by the mutation of a single gene. In common disorders, a number of genetic abnormalities must occur in combination or in conjunction with particular environmental influences in order for the genetic abnormality to be "expressed"—that is, to result in the patient actually bearing the disorder. Some genetic abnormalities, therefore, never cause actual disease, if the other necessary genetic or environmental causes do not occur.

Even if the necessary combinations of genetic or environmental events are present in sufficient measure for the disease to be manifest, the severity may vary dramatically. Effects may range from mild symptoms to severe health consequences, and the age when they first appear also may vary from childhood to late adulthood. Therefore, even the detection of a genetic abnormality by a "predictive" genetic test leaves the subject with crucial and inherent uncertainties about whether the disease will become manifest, how mild or severe its effects may be, and how early or late in life they may occur.

Ultimately, advances in the understanding of genetic influences on disease may result in therapies that can prevent these ailments. Before therapies are developed, though, the discovery of disease-related genes will result in tests that determine the probability either of genetic disease or genetic susceptibility to disease. Clinical trials of a genetic test for cystic fibrosis are under way, and one for predisposition to colon cancer has been announced. Prior to the discovery of therapies for genetically influenced diseases, predictive tests may allow earlier and more effective medical interventions for persons with increased genetic susceptibility to some diseases. Identification of persons with a genetic predisposition to colon and/or breast cancer or heart disease, for example, may reduce their risk of serious illness through lifestyle regimens, elimination of contributing environmental factors, earlier and more frequent diagnostic tests, and sooner detection and treatment when disease does begin to occur.

Non-Medical Usage

The medical benefits of predictive genetic testing are likely to be accompanied by problematic consequences from the non-medical uses of increased genetic information. Genetic risk information could be used by cost-sensitive employers to deny or restrict persons access-to health insurance, employee health benefits, or even jobs and advancement opportunities. With such serious consequences at stake, great care must be exercised in the development of public policies to protect individuals who are vulnerable to unwarranted discrimination on the basis of genetic risk factors.

Since the results of denying someone access to a job or health care benefits may be dire, only information from genetic tests with negligible rates of false-positive identification (when a medical test falsely identifies the subject as positive for having the disease gene) should be allowed for non-medical uses such as exclusions from employment or insurance. Although the Americans with Disabilities Act of 1990 (ADA) may be interpreted to prevent employers from discriminating on the basis of genetic predisposition to disease, it clearly allows them to base hiring decisions on disabilities, including manifest genetic disorders, if they can not be "reasonably accommodated" or if they endanger public safety. Therefore, genetic tests used to justify such exceptions to the ADA ban on disability-based distinctions should be held to the highest possible standards of validity.

Moreover, even though the ADA prevents employers from considering certain medical information in hiring decisions, it is allowed to be considered in insurance coverage. The importance of employer-based health insurance in access to medical care reinforces the need to restrict insurers' use of information to those genetic tests that do not have unacceptable rates of false-positive identification.

Informed consent is a paramount requirement for all types of medical treatment, not merely genetic testing. The non-medical uses for genetic tests require a broader than usual scope of informed consent. The subject clearly must be advised not only of the medical consequences of the test, but also the non-medical ones, such as the potential impact on employability or health care benefits. Physicians must disclose both the medical and non-medical consequences of genetic test information *before* administering such tests, so that patients may weigh the medical and personal benefits against adverse consequences that may result from use by employers, insurers, or other interested parties.

Genuine informed consent must allow the patient a real chance to accept or refuse the test or procedure. In order to be valid in any meaningful sense, informed consent must be truly voluntary, free of undue influence, coercion, abuse, or disproportionate bargaining power by the party offering, administering, or urging the test. In view of an individual's perceived need for employment or health care coverage, conditioning a job or health benefits on submission to genetic tests is likely to exert a coercive influence that undermines the voluntariness of informed consent. Thus, employers, unions, and insurers should not be allowed to require applicants to undergo a genetic test as a condition of obtaining health care coverage or benefits. However, if proposed health care finance reforms do not achieve universal coverage for everyone, it may be necessary to allow insurers access to the results of genetic tests freely requested by patients in order to prevent some individuals from buying or increasing insurance coverage only after they learn from a genetic test of an imminent likelihood of serious disease.

Appropriate informed consent for genetic tests will be more likely to occur in the context of medical care by health care providers than by employers, insurers, and other parties that are not disinterested. All of the information necessary to a balanced consideration of the benefits and burdens of learning test results are more likely to be provided in the context of medical care than in an insurance application.

Of course, health care practitioners are not entirely disinterested. They, too, may have incentives to promote genetic tests that indirectly may compromise appropriate informed consent. In a fee-for-service setting, providers have a direct financial incentive to recommend genetic tests. Alternatively, in a managed care system, in which providers save money by preventive steps that minimize late-stage acute care, physicians have an incentive to recommend genetic tests aggressively to allow earlier intervention and less expensive courses of treatment.

Although these incentives may coincide with some patient

interests, other valid personal considerations legitimately may affect individuals' decisions and should not be unduly overridden by overzealous advocacy of genetic testing. These respective incentives for health care providers to push genetic tests must be countered by strict adherence to physicians' fiduciary duty to patients' rights and by respect for patients' complete autonomy on the issue of informed consent for genetic testing.

Confidentiality of Genetic Information

As for the implications for genetic testing, both the current system of health care financing and the multitude of people with direct access to patients' records, especially in institutional settings, seriously compromise the traditional notion of medical confidentiality. Scores of persons in such institutions may have legitimate access to a patient's records. In addition, the automated information systems in which medical records are contained compound the potential for breaches of confidential data and unauthorized replication of it.

Most insurance forms contain blanket release clauses that, if signed by the insured, permit the insurers to obtain and distribute to other insurers whatever material they deem relevant to a consumer's risk or the validity of a claim. Most people who sign such releases are unaware of the extent of insurer investigation and distribution of information or of the risks entailed in it. The reliability of the data obtained by insurers may not be adequately or independently verified. Such information may be replicated in more than one data base. This makes it difficult to correct inaccuracies, because those involved do not know that the information exists, are unaware of procedures to correct it, and are not cognizant of additional data banks wherein it may be found.

Compromising the confidentiality of genetic information could have serious consequences for employment and health care coverage. In addition, the risk of stigmatization makes genetic information especially sensitive. In one study of a Mediterranean population, general awareness of an individual's genetic status affected his or her chances of marriage, even though the real risks were exaggerated or misunderstood. Breaching the confidentiality of genetic information may have adverse consequences not only for the individual who has been tested, but also for family members, whether or not such implications are accurate.

In order to protect the confidentiality of genetic information, medical record systems—especially the coordinated, automated ones characteristic of current health care—should be designed or retrofitted with sophisticated safeguards to prevent access to confidential medical information. Health data systems maintained by commercial insurers, self-insured groups, government entities, and all other third-party payers should be required to initiate and publicize reliable methods of reviewing, challenging, deleting, and correcting inaccurate or unauthorized genetic information. The insurance industry's primary data clearinghouse,

"Most people who sign such releases are unaware of the extent of insurer investigation and distribution of information..."

the Medical Information Bureau (MIB), has procedures for consumers to review and challenge their records. Most people, though, are not aware of these measures, and the releases signed by applicants allow releases of information outside the MIB's procedures. Since the MIB is an insurance industry association, some appeal process of last resort should be developed that is independent of the organizations or industry that maintains the information in question.

Even without the advent of widespread predictive genetic testing, approximately 37,000,000 Americans are uninsured and a comparable amount are underinsured for the health care they are most likely to need. The introduction of predictive genetic testing to the current health care financing system likely would increase the numbers of the uninsured and underinsured. Currently, a person who has a serious health condition is likely to be denied insurance, charged unaffordable premiums, or covered for everything other than the existing disorder the next time he or she changes coverage, which may occur frequently in a system that reconsiders health risks every time an insured individual changes employers. People already are subject to denial, premium surcharges, or coverage exclusions on the basis of health problems that have occurred since they last changed coverage. If they similarly were weeded out for their risk of future disease based on predictive genetic tests, even more would be likely to experience roadblocks to health care coverage.

"People already are subject to denial, premium surcharges, or coverage exclusions on the basis of health problems..."

The prospect that widespread use of predictive genetic tests will result in reduced health coverage reinforces the necessity of health care reform characterized by universal coverage for everyone, as well as community rating, in which premium rates are not based on exclusion of persons with the highest risks and, therefore, the greatest needs. Although the shape of health care reform is uncertain, it appears that the Clinton Administration will continue to push for universal coverage. Genetic testing's potential to provoke exclusions from coverage makes it important to curtail the competitive incentives to bar higher-risk individuals.

In the Clinton plan, universal coverage is likely to include a basic package of comprehensive health benefits. Several important features of such a system must be addressed to ensure that genetic discrimination in health care coverage does not occur. According to the theory of managed competition on which proposed reforms are based, the basic benefit package should entail comprehensive care offered by plans competing on the basis of efficient delivery, rather than to eliminate the higher risk from their coverage. If the managed competition idea works, excluding people from coverage based on medical risk likely will be minimal.

If the basic benefit package is not sufficiently comprehensive, however, requiring some benefits—such as certain surgeries, long-term care, or prescription drugs—to be bought with supplemental insurance premiums, those with evidence of substantial future medical needs and costs would be forced to buy supplemental insurance. If this happens, the market once again could become segmented according to medical risk. If the basic package does not cover adequately genetic testing, counseling, and other important genetic services, the issues arising from genetic discrimination will be shifted to the supplemental insurance market. If this were to occur, the problems of lack of access to medical care could resurface for individuals with genetic susceptibilities to disease.

All health care financing entities in the reformed health care system should be required to pay for or provide genetic testing that gives cost-beneficial information to patients. People should not be forced to undergo genetic testing as a condition of membership in the insurance or benefit plan, or for purposes of establishing a premium structure based on medical risk. If some plans institute genetic testing programs designed to achieve health promotion or cost-efficiency goals, they should provide a clearly disclosed means for all enrolled persons to make an informed refusal of testing on grounds of privacy rights, religious beliefs, or other conscientious objections.

In the long run, the imminent advances in genetic understanding should bring improvements in medical treatment. Care must be taken to ensure that these gains in diagnostic and therapeutic medicine are not marred by a simultaneous erosion of patients', employees', and insurance consumers' rights to informed consent and confidentiality. A health care financing system must not penalize people for genetically inherited tendencies to disease that are beyond their ability to choose or overcome.

IV. Cyberspace Controversies

Editor's Introduction

The fourth and final section of this issue of the *Reference Shelf* centers on electronic privacy concerns. In an opening article from *Business Week*, Catherine Yang comments on Congress's interest in regulating cyberspace, including the appointment of Christine A. Varney, a member of the Federal Trade Commission, as an overseer to protect consumers who buy products and services online against fraud, deceptive ads, and privacy violations. One of her assignments will be to set up safeguards against marketers plundering electronic messages for personal data. Additional privacy concerns include the sale of E-mail addresses to marketers sending solicitations on the Internet. As Yang notes, the upcoming contest for regulating the industry will be between the government and industry officials themselves.

In the following article from *The Progressive*, Erik Ness discusses the National Information Infrastructure, or the information superhighway, which will, it is claimed, eventually connect every home and business in the United States and the world to an ever growing web of electronic services. But, Ness warns, this "potential global village" could reflect George Orwell's *1984*. On the one hand, it offers an open field for those who collect and sell personal data, thus posing a serious erosion of privacy; on the other hand, attempts to regulate it—to impose censorship—would put society under the thumb of "Big Brother." The latter part of the article deals with the Clinton administration's Clipper chip proposal that would supposedly ensure privacy protection for electronic communications while preserving the government's ability to conduct authorized wiretaps.

The Clipper Chip question is also addressed by Dorothy Denning in her article from *Technology Review*. Denning writes as an advocate for the Clipper Chip program, which would make use of "key-escrow" encryption. Under this plan, an essentially "unbreakable" encryption scheme would be made broadly available, but it could be decoded by special keys held in escrow by the federal government at the National Institute of Standards and Technology and the Treasury Department's Automated Systems Division. Denning's case is well stated, but it tends to downplay the risks to freedom and privacy that the scheme might impose. For this reason, in fact, the Clipper Chip idea failed to win broad support. Steven Levy's article on the Clipper Chip in the *New York Times Magazine* is a superb piece of writing, which provides the complicated history of the Clipper Chip controversy with clarity and suspenseful precision. A special feature of the article is his description of the "crypto war" between government proponents of the Clipper Chip and the "cypberpunks," the most admired of whom, Philip R. Zimmerman, created a dazzlingly formidable encryption that he called PGP ("Pretty Good Privacy").

The concluding article in this section, by Sara Curtis in *Maclean's*, concerns the much discussed issue of pornography on the Internet, and what to do about it. In February 1996, President Clinton signed into law a sweeping telecommunications bill that imposes fines of up to $340,000 and as long as five years in prison for transmitting "indecent material" over a public computer network to which minors have access. This legislation has already been contested by the ACLU as a violation of free speech. In the meantime software programs have become available either advising parents where the objectionable material is found, or enabling them to "filter" it out with a special device if they wish.

How Do You Police Cyberspace?[1]

To the dismay of seasoned net surfers, government arrived in freewheeling cyberspace last year with a heavy hand. Congress proposed to jail anyone sending smut online. A federal judge ruled against Prodigy Services Inc. for libel. And abroad, German authorities barred CompuServe Inc. from offering sites containing pornography. Internet pioneers were outraged at the intrusions.

But as cyberspace increasingly becomes a medium of social transaction and commerce, government efforts to regulate it are sure to increase. Enter Christine A. Varney, 40, the youngest member of the Federal Trade Commission. Her mission: To become the first U. S. Cyber-Marshall, protecting consumers buying products and services online against fraud, deceptive ads, and privacy violations. "The laws on the books should exist in cyberspace, too," she says.

Varney, a Clinton appointee who joined the FTC in October, 1994, insists she isn't about to strangle the burgeoning technology with rules. "As a New Democrat, I believe we don't know nearly enough to regulate now," she says. That's why she endorses industry self-policing as a first step. In September, she inaugurated the FTC's Privacy Initiative, inviting consumers, online service companies, advertisers, and others to propose voluntary industry guidelines to protect the privacy of Internet users by spring. To get the dialogue going, the FTC has established a Web site, which has logged almost 200 comments so far.

Cyber-snooping is not big business yet. But with electronic marketing expected to take off this year, Varney is heeding predictions that consumers will clamor for more safeguards against marketers culling personal data from their virtual communications. In the meantime, the former partner at the Washington law firm of Hogan & Hartson has spurred FTC probes into alleged fraud and misleading advertising in cyberspace. Several cases— including actions against advertising in the guise of anonymous online testimonials—will be unveiled this spring.

Varney is no stranger to the Brave Net World. As former Cabinet Secretary for the Clinton White House, her job was to monitor and coordinate communications among the Administration's agency chiefs. But the longtime cybersurfer was shocked that her wards didn't have E-mail and pushed to get them wired.

UNLIKELY ALLIES. Now her go-slow attitude on regulation worries privacy rights advocates. The FTC has "adopted a see-no-

---

[1] Article by Catherine Yang, staffwriter from *Business Week* 97-8 F 26, '96. Copyright © 1996 The McGraw-Hill Companies, Inc. Reprinted with permission.

evil, hear-no-evil strategy," complains Mark Rotenberg, director of the Electronic Privacy Information Center. "Because the FTC is not prepared to protect privacy, there will be tremendous waffling" in the industry.

But Varney has support from some unlikely allies, who share her fear that tight regulation of the Net may be premature. "You don't want to regulate this new frontier to death before giving it a chance to live and flourish," says Richard F. O'Donnell, spokesman for the Progress & Freedom Foundation, a conservative think tank allied with House Speaker Newt Gingrich. And many in the Net *avant garde* agree. "We're in the age of the Stanley Steamer trying to figure out how I-95 is going to work in 50 years," says D. C. attorney Ronald Plesser.

"...electronic privacy concerns center on the sale of E-mail addresses to marketers interested in sending solicitations via the Net."

While Varney believes the FTC can police online fraud and deceptive ads through traditional enforcement, she thinks protecting privacy will create the greatest challenge for regulators because fast-changing technology presents totally new ways for business to observe consumers' habits. For example, marketers may soon be able to track someone's "clickstream"—the areas in cyberspace that a consumer clicks on to with a mouse, including all Web sites visited, pages accessed, and time spent per page. That could provide a starkly revealing glimpse of an Internet user. Given such possibilities, "we do need to exercise some self-control," says Roland J. Sharette, vice-president at J. Walter Thompson USA in Detroit, which represents online advertisers including Ford Motor, Motorola, and Kodak.

For now, electronic privacy concerns center on the sale of E-mail addresses to marketers interested in sending solicitations via the Net. A handful of mailing-list brokers have recently launched E-mail businesses. Altoona (Pa.)-based net.net advertising inc., for example, is about to rent a list of 1 million E-mail addresses collected from the Net to four large corporations, including Shell Oil Co. Net.net is clipping the list into 100 interest categories—including sports, arts, and investments. But the company claims to protect privacy by allowing consumers to opt out of the mailing list—similar to a database maintained by the Direct Marketing Assn. that allows consumers to avoid receiving snail-mail solicitations.

Privacy Edge. Cyber-marketers recognize that such protections might lure more consumers into electronic transactions—from shopping to banking. "If you don't respect privacy, the industry is not going to grow," says William J. Tobin, president of Oakton (Va.)-based PC Flowers & Gifts Inc., a pioneering online marketer. And guaranteeing privacy may give one online service provider an edge over others. "Consumers are starting to shop around," notes Bill Burrington, assistant general counsel at America Online Inc. in Vienna, Va.

Still, online service companies are unlikely to give up the revenues they're getting from selling information about their subscribers to marketers. AOL and CompuServe sell such data, and Prodigy will send messages to targeted subscribers on behalf of advertisers.

But the industry realizes it has to come up with its own rules of the road—at least to stave off burgeoning attempts by the states to regulate online privacy. The online service companies successfully scuttled a proposal introduced in Maryland last fall requiring them to give subscribers the opportunity at least every year to opt out of receiving unsolicited E-mail. Now, a Minnesota lawmaker is contemplating introducing a measure prohibiting online service providers from giving out personal information about their users without their consent.

The industry has just begun to devise minimum privacy standards under the auspices of the Interactive Services Assn.—which may offer on-screen options for consumers to click on to bar the use of personal data. But some businesses balk at rules they say would put them at a disadvantage to other industries. For example, if E-mailing your personal shopper at Nordstrom's entails lots of time-consuming questions aimed at securing consumer consent on private information, you might simply use the telephone. "Erecting huge numbers of roadblocks becomes burdensome for E-mail-based transactions," says William R. Moroney, president of Multimedia Telecommunications Assn., which represents phone and computer technology companies.

An even greater challenge is the global nature of the technology. "We could run our company off a sailboat in the middle of the ocean," says Philip E. Devorris, net.net's president. "I don't know how you could police it."

Even Varney admits that her initial moves at cyber-regulation are just the beginning of a long process. "I don't think self-regulation ultimately will provide all the answers," she says, envisioning a time when the government may have to adopt more aggressive rules. "But it's a good start." Varney only hopes that in the end, both technology and consumers win.

"...a Minnesota lawmaker is contemplating introducing a measure prohibiting online service providers from giving out personal information...."

Big Brother@Cyberspace[2]

In its popular series of futuristic commercials, AT&T paints a liberating picture of your not-too-distant life, when the information superhighway will be an instrument of personal freedom and a servant to your worldly needs and desires. But is the future of cyberspace really so elegant, so convenient? Or does it represent a serious threat to your privacy and your freedom?

The information superhighway is at least a decade away for most of us, but whether you know it or not, you already exist in cyberspace—through credit and other electronic records, your phone line, and your cable television. Constitutional scholar Laurence Tribe has argued that "without further thought and awareness...the danger is clear and present" that the Constitution's core values will be compromised "in the dim reaches of cyberspace."

When you visit your doctor, it is increasingly likely that your medical records are kept on a computer. Many of the health-care bills introduced in Congress this year called for a national medical database to link these records. Unfortunately, law-enforcement officers could gain access to those files without even obtaining a warrant. President Nixon's henchmen had to break into Daniel Ellsberg's psychiatrist's office to pull his files. Using a national medical database, they would need only to press a button.

Of course, the Government already has large stores of sensitive personal information at its disposal. In July of this year, Senator John Glenn, Ohio Democrat, released Internal Revenue Service papers showing that its employees were using IRS computers to prowl through the tax files of family, friends, neighbors, and celebrities. Since 1989, the IRS says, the agency has investigated more than 1,300 of its employees for unauthorized browsing; more than 400 employees have been disciplined.

But even seemingly benign information—your address in a government computer, for example—can betray you. Chris Criner volunteers as an escort for an abortion clinic in Tustin, California. After a Saturday morning of escort work in November 1992, Criner returned home to find a note on his door reading, "Hi. We came by for coffee. We'll be back." One week later, Operation Rescue picketed his apartment. Criner was mystified; after clinic work he always went shopping or took a different route home to shake any over-zealous pursuers.

Criner had noticed a new protester lately—a man scribbling notes on a clipboard. Then one protester asked about Criner's wife, a clinic worker, using her given name—not the one she was

[2] Article by Erik Ness, editor of The Progressive Media Project, from *The Progressive* 58:22-7 D '94. Copyright © 1994 *The Progressive* Madison, WI. Reprinted with permission.

known by. On a hunch, Criner and others at the clinic filed a complaint with the California Department of Motor Vehicles and found that four of their license plates had been illegally traced within an hour of each other at the Anaheim Police Department.

A former police employee eventually confessed to intruding into the restricted files. But Criner is still chilled by the incident—particularly after the shooting deaths of two abortion providers and a clinic escort in Pensacola, Florida. "Who knows where this information went besides this one little picket group?" he wonders. "Maybe it's on a computer bulletin board somewhere, or in some militant prolife newsletter. Should I worry about my wife getting shot in the back of the head as she walks up to our front door because they know where we live?"

Businesses, government officials, activists, engineers, and intellectuals are busily defining cyberspace, and with various goals. Their divergent interests meet on the National Information Infrastructure, the so-called information superhighway. This cable—capable of delivering voice, data, and video images at high speed—is eventually supposed to connect every home and business in the United States and the world to an ever-growing web of electronic services ranging from stock quotations to movies on demand. The buzzword for this change is "convergence"—the melding of telephone, computer, and television technologies into the foundation of an information economy.

The Clinton Administration, particularly Vice President Al Gore, is a self-proclaimed champion of this information age. The business world is salivating over potential profits in the information economy. Meanwhile, consumer advocates and privacy experts warn that, without proper safeguards, this potential global village could become George Orwell's *1984*.

The National Information Infrastructure is projected to cost between $400 billion and $700 billion. During the 1992 Presidential campaign, Gore called for a major Government role in its development, but high Federal debt has led the Administration to favor private-sector design and operation instead. This shift has placed an even bigger burden on Congressional efforts this year to restructure the nation's $170 billion telecommunications industry, consisting of local telephone companies (worth $90 billion), long-distance carriers ($60 billion), and cable television industry (worth $20 billion).

The basic goal was to allow phone and cable operators to compete with each other locally, while preventing a total monopoly of both by any one company in one area and developing a new definition of universal service. Regulators and activists alike have long been leery of allowing a monopoly of the wires going into the American home, and their apprehensions have been heightened as electronic communication and commerce increasingly become central parts of our lives.

But even as telephone companies and cable television were eager to compete with each other for emerging markets, their rivalry got the better of them, killing telecommunications restructuring in the Senate. "Much of this battle is over who will control the television of the future," explains Jeff Chester of the Washington-based Center for Media Education. One example, he says, was NBC's effort to create a competitor for Ted Turner's twenty-four-hour Cable News Network. John Malone, president of TCI—who has a financial stake in CNN—controlled enough of the cable market that he was able to force NBC to turn a hard-news service into a softer, infotainment-oriented channel. "Their principal focus is profit, not the currency of democracy, not the diversity of ideas," warns Chester.

"We're in real danger of having a handful of giant, global communications corporations controlling the public mind," says Chester, whose organization filed a thirty-eight-page brief with the FCC opposing last year's mega-deal between Bell Atlantic and cable giant Telecommunications, Inc. The deal broke down, but that has not slowed the pace of consolidation: In the last year, AirTouch Communication acquired U.S. West (a deal worth $13.5 billion), AT&T Corporation merged with McCaw Cellular Communications, Inc. (a $12.6 billion value), and Viacom bought Blockbuster Entertainment ($7.97 billion).

"There is a direct relationship between the health of our democracy and the diversity of our communications system," says Chester. "I think one reason why the body politic is so ill can be traced back to problems with the media system and the institutions which are part of it."

If we're not careful, he says, today's captive consumer of telephone and cable television will become tomorrow's totally exposed consumer.

"We're turning over the info superhighway to Madison Avenue, so they can better, more effectively serve the needs of advertisers to target individuals in discrete demographic groups."

As if to emphasize this, no sooner had the telecommunications restructuring bill died for the year than the computer service America Online ignited a fresh battle in cyberspace when it advertised its "upscale" subscriber list in a direct-mail trade publication. "America Online members are computer and modem owners who pay up to $200 a month to enjoy hundreds of entertaining and informative services," the ad promised. "Credit-worthy—over 85 per cent pay by credit card.... Mail Order Buyers!"

The popular online service drew fire from Massachusetts Representative Edward Markey, chairman of the House Subcommittee on Telecommunications and Finance, who fired off a letter to America Online president Steve Case, arguing that "comprehensive privacy protections must become part of the electronic ethics of companies doing business on the information superhighway and a fundamental right of all its travelers."

According to David Banisar, staff attorney for the Electronic Privacy Information Center, the America Online controversy is important because commerce on the Internet is in danger of becoming more like a shopping mall than a public street. "In shopping malls, the owners can pretty much do what they want," he warns, "and those same shopping malls are going to be collecting reams, if I can use an old-fashioned term, of personal data." With more transactions taking place over the net, more personal information about you enters cyberspace. "Even if you go into a store," says Banisar, "the odds are it's going to transfer transaction information via the same superhighway to its suppliers, to its deliverers, and to its main offices."

America Online was not unique. As Case pointed out, CompuServe, another online service, had been renting its list for years. In fact, the mailing-list business is a refined industry; lists can include explicit and implicit demographic information ranging from income to political preferences to your favorite television shows. But these are relatively primitive compared to what advancing computer technology could produce: complete profiles of consumers, including brand-name inclinations, credit histories, and shopping habits. Many supermarkets already use checkcashing cards that, in conjunction with computerized scanners, keep detailed records of consumer spending habits. Will your insurance company someday be able to learn whether or not you buy beer and cigarettes?

First Amendment rights are already at issue in cyberspace. One major concern is whether commercial online companies deserve the broad protection of telephone companies, which have no responsibility for the content of conversations on their wires, and bookstores, which are also broadly protected, or are like publishers and broadcasters, who are held accountable for libel and other transgressions.

CompuServe, the oldest and largest online service, appears to want it both ways. In 1990, an online journal called Rumorville, produced under contract for CompuServe, published allegedly defamatory remarks about a competitor, Skuttlebut. When Skuttlebut sued for libel in a New York district court, CompuServe argued that it was more like a bookstore than a publisher, and therefore subject to a different standard of libel. The court agreed, saying a "computerized database is the functional equivalent of a more traditional news vendor." Because it did not exercise control over editorial content, it was not held liable for defamation.

But last year, CompuServe took a different approach toward Richard Patterson, a computer programmer and CompuServe member who believes—and claimed online—that the company had infringed on his trademark.

CompuServe asked a Federal court to resolve the trademark dispute, but warned Patterson that if he discussed the suit online it would sever his CompuServe access.

This contradictory strategy indicates the general confusion over what rights and privileges are accorded in the commercial online environment.

"Many supermarkets already use checkcashing cards that, in conjunction with computerized scanners, keep detailed records of consumer spending habits."

Because the services are private, they are not automatically obligated to respect constitutional rights of privacy and freedom of expression.

Several years ago, Prodigy, another service, booted subscribers who tried to fight a rate hike, and censored anti-Semitic comments in online forums. Just this year, America Online closed several feminist discussion forums for fear that young girls might stumble upon adult discussions.

Censorship can take insidious forms online. Users do not always understand the different regions of cyberspace, which is divided into loosely overlapping sectors ranging from the commercial services to the Internet to underground bulletin boards trafficking in stolen credit card numbers. Usenet, for example, is a sprawling electronic forum with more than 8,000 discussion groups ranging from alt.fan. Noam Chomsky to alt.tv-dinosaurs.barney.die.die.die.

"...communication on the net is often hailed for its casual intelligence...."

CompuServe and America Online both offer access to Usenet, but restrict areas—largely those dealing with sexuality—that they deem objectionable. On CompuServe, you can't subscribe to a newsgroup deemed objectionable by the company unless you know the exact title. Since many people choose their newsgroups by scanning for key words, the company automatically reserves full access for the initiated. America Online does not provide access at all to what it decides are objectionable groups.

Both companies promised to provide me with the list of excluded discussion groups, but did not.

Less-restricted portions of the net are also censored, though generally with a lighter touch. Working within established and respected community guidelines, some Usenet groups are moderated to keep discussions focused. It's easy to appreciate the utility of the policy—communication on the net is often hailed for its casual intelligence and its potential to build community. But if every keystroke of every person who had ever surfed the net were saved in perpetuity, it would quickly drown in its own chatter.

Of more immediate concern these days is the increasingly unruly environment as new members unfamiliar with traditions flood the net. The Internet actually began as a military research project, but when scientists discovered its usefulness for exchanging data and computer power, the National Science Foundation took over administration. It grew largely unregulated into what has been called the largest functioning anarchy, with users establishing protocols and "netiquette."

Within this intellectual framework of self-governance, the move toward commercialism has met vociferous resistance. Last April, the Phoenix immigration law firm of Canter & Segal advertised its services on Usenet by placing messages in thousands of forums, the vast majority of which had no relationship to immigration. While informational postings in related areas have been tolerated on Usenet, the indiscriminate Canter & Segal posting drew a furious response. Outraged "netizens" deluged the company with angry e-mail messages called "flames." Undeterred by the communal outrage, Cantor & Sogal ventured onto the net again in June, drawing the ire of a Norwegian programmer who devised a search-and-destroy program, or "cancelbot" to wipe out the firm's transmissions. As the net becomes more crowded and contentious, the specter of vigilante censors seems quite real.

Despite the phenomenal growth of computer networks, relatively few people are actually online. Some five million subscribe to commercial services, while as many as twenty million gain access to the Internet through universities or work. Online computing has sparked such interest because it is the most likely model for the emerging information economy.

In the future, your telephone, computer, and television will all be linked, and you'll gain access to everything from the latest rap video to maps of Virginia in the 1600s stored in the Library of Congress, using the kinds of graphical interfaces being pioneered by America Online and CompuServe.

"Online computing has sparked such interest because it is the most likely model for the emerging information economy."

But while the media hype a Golden Age of democracy spurred by the free flow of information, commercial online services resemble nothing so much as the current offerings of television and newsstands: *Time*, *The Atlantic*, ABC, DC Comics, the *Chicago Tribune*, Associated Press, and Reuters.

What would it take for a publication like *The Progressive* to get online? Brian Jaffe, director of online publications for CompuServe, the country's largest commercial online service, is firm about its priorities. "We're in business to make money," he explains. "The overall tone is going to be: You have to sell me on you."

First, *The Progressive* would have to show CompuServe that it would "add value to the service" by providing the demographic makeup of the people it was planning to reach online. Second, Jaffe looks at brand-name awareness. "When you pop up in our WHAT'S NEW—our intrusive marketing area—and I see *The Progressive* is online, come visit our area, I don't know what type of emotion that's going to stir in our two-and-a-quarter million users." Finally, Jaffe looks at "co-marketing opportunities"— basically, what kind of new members *The Progressive* would offer to CompuServe—an evaluation driven by circulation and demographics. "We are an extremely powerful marketing entity," says Jaffe, citing CompuServe's phenomenal growth rate of 85,000 new members a month. Next to this, *The Progressive*'s 32,000 circulation is relatively small, a factor that he says doesn't work in its favor.

Still, you may yet find publications like *The Progressive* available from commercial online services. "I'm never going to turn a deaf ear, because I never know when the next winner is going to come around," says Jaffe. But, he cautions, "You're right, we don't have a lot of political-type publications online. To be quite honest with you—maybe you can convince me otherwise—but it doesn't quite fit in with the publishing formula that I'm looking for in a successful online product."

The clout of these commercial services already intimidates small publications. As a staff member from one alternative periodical said after discussing its efforts to get online, "Don't say anything about us being critical of them that could hurt their willingness to sign us on in the future."

This clout will only increase as the Internet moves from the public to the private sector. More than half of it is now commercial in origin, and the National Science Foundation is passing management of the remainder into private hands. The Internet has thrived in part because its flat-rate pricing has made it possible for individuals and nonprofits to take full advantage of electronic communications. Eventually, the net will abandon flat-rate pricing, which could curtail open participation as costs rise. The booming media interest in the Internet may also be more cloud than silver lining: "It's clear to me the media industries want to use the Internet as another programming channel that they control," says Chester.

"The Internet has thrived in part because its flat-rate pricing has made it possible for individuals and nonprofits to take full advantage of electronic communications."

While the Clinton Administration has won praise for its information-age advocacy, it has taken a beating on privacy. "The Clinton Administration has paid some lip service to privacy issues, but it's really done almost nothing," explains Dave Banisar of the Electronic Privacy Information Center.

Bill Clinton's first mistake was the hugely unpopular Clipper chip proposal. Clipper is a computer chip that scrambles a message using a classified mathematical function.

Users would have numerical keys to encode and decode messages, but two agencies—the Treasury Department and the National Institute of Standards and Technology—would hold copies of the keys in escrow, providing Government access as needed. Clipper was the response of law-enforcement and national-security officials who see cheap and powerful computers making it easier for criminals and spies to break the law.

Many cryptographers worried that Clipper, classified and developed in secret by the National Security Agency, might not be secure, and would not sufficiently protect privacy. To get your key, law officers would not have to present a warrant—they would only have to fax a request claiming they had a warrant. Safeguards against dissemination of the key and guaranteeing destruction once the order had expired were also deemed insufficient.

The keys for every Clipper chip would be available to only a handful of people, but if these individuals were corrupted, the whole system would be compromised. NSA involvement also worried some people: Had the agency built a trapdoor into the system that would allow it special access?

Even the Office of Technology Assessment criticized the agency's involvement in Clipper, concluding it was "part of a long-term control strategy intended to retard the general availability of 'unbreakable' or 'hard-to-break' cryptography within the United States."

Clipper has been essentially abandoned for data encryption, but is still on the table as a standard for voice encryption. Gore is currently working to develop a compromise, but has said that the White House will not yield on the proposed key escrow, though the Government would not have to be the escrow agent.

Clipper is only one part of vigorous efforts by the authorities to protect their eavesdropping rights. "If you think crime is bad now, just wait and see what happens if the FBI one day is no longer able to conduct court-approved electronic surveillance," FBI director Louis Freeh told an audience last May soon after the reintroduction of his agency's Digital Telephony in Congress.

First proposed by the Bush Administration and one of the few bills successfully pushed through the last Congress by Clinton, digital telephony requires common carriers—telephone companies—to help law-enforcement officers with appropriate court orders to listen to your conversations. It would also make transactional data—who's calling whom—easily available to law-enforcement officers. To do this, the phone companies need special equipment to ensure access to their new digital switches—equipment the legislation would buy for $500 million.

But is this cost-effective law enforcement? Freeh testified before the Senate in March that not a single wiretap order has been hindered by advancing technology. Since the 1968 passage of wiretap legislation, there have been about 900 Federal and state wiretaps per year, costing an average of $46,492 per tap in 1992.

Why should law-abiding citizens be concerned with wiretaps, codes, and scrambled conversations? The British royal family is certainly the most public example of the hazards of unsecured communications, but Philip Zimmermann, a cryptographic-software designer, told Congress last year that technological advances made possible massive Government intrusions on privacy. "Today," Zimmermann warned, "electronic mail is gradually replacing conventional paper mail, and is soon to be the norm for everyone, not the novelty it is today.

"Unlike paper mail," he added, "e-mail messages are just too easy to intercept and scan for interesting key words. This can be done easily, routinely, automatically, and undetectably on a grand scale. This is analogous to drift net fishing—making a quantitative and qualitative Orwellian difference to the health of democracy."

Among the rationales for increased electronic-monitoring powers is the need to fight computer crime. Law-enforcement officials cite a burgeoning traffic in pornography, illegally copied software, and stolen credit information, but often they have been too trigger-happy in policing a world they don't fully understand. Specific targets have been computer bulletin boards, which people dial into to obtain information or to talk.

Police in Munroe Falls, Ohio, confiscated the $3,000 computer of Mark Lehrer, charging that kids had seen pornography on his bulletin board, Akron Anomaly. Lehrer did have some X-rated files, but access was restricted—users had to send a copy of their driver's license to get in.

A few explicit photos were in common space—Lehrer claims a filing error—so local police recruited a fifteen-year-old to gain access to the files, then busted Lehrer. But with no complaints from local parents, the charge didn't stick. Police filed new charges alleging that other photos—not even available on the bulletin board, but seized with the computer—could have depicted minors.

Lacking the money for expert testimony, Lehrer entered a guilty plea to a misdemeanor charge of possessing a criminal tool—his computer. But confiscating the computer for a misfiled picture is akin to seizing a convenience store for a misfiled copy of Penthouse. An Akron Beacon editorial asked "whether the police were protecting against a child pornographer or using the intimidating powers of the police and judicial system to help themselves to a nice hunk of expensive machinery."

Michael Elansky ran the Ware House bulletin board in West Hartford, Connecticut. Elansky was arrested in August 1993, when police found files on his bulletin board explaining in detail the construction of various explosive devices. The files had been written four years earlier by a fifteen-year-old, and contained constitutionally protected information widely available in sources ranging from chemistry textbooks to The Anarchist Cookbook.

Elansky's case was compounded by his previous scrapes with the law—he eventually entered guilty pleas to parole violation—but the charges relating to the bulletin board files were never dropped.

Activists maintain that his arrest and detention (Elansky could not post the $500,000 bond) were a violation of First Amendment rights and do not bode well for free speech in cyberspace.

"I don't think it's a police conspiracy to chill the whole net," says Banisar of such crackdowns, "but it certainly has that result." Banisar says the most closely watched legal contest in cyberspace is that of Robert Alan Thomas and his wife, Carleen, who live in Milpitas, California, where they ran the Amateur Action Bulletin Board Service.

Subscribers—3,600 in the United States and Europe—paid $99 a year, using their computers to call the Amateur Action computer and download pornographic photographs, chat with other members, and order explicit videotapes.

Then a Tennessee hacker broke into the system. Disturbed by the hard-core content, the intruder alerted the Memphis authorities, who began a sting operation. The Thomases were busted and saddled with eleven Federal obscenity charges—not in California but in Tennessee, the heart of the Bible belt. For the first time a bulletin-board operator was prosecuted where the obscene material was received instead of at its point of origin. The Thomases were convicted; the case is on appeal and could end up in the Supreme Court.

At issue is the Supreme Court's 1973 ruling that obscenity be judged by local community standards. This time, the Court would have to answer a new question: Where are you when you're in cyberspace? "Whatever your view of looking at nudie pictures, this is pretty chilling for everybody in the rest of the country that doesn't want to be subject to Tennessee morals," says David Banisar of the Electronic Privacy Information Center.

"If I wanted to be subject to Tennessee morals, I'd move to Tennessee."

Just as Al Gore is playing an important role in the National Information Infrastructure, his father helped create the interstate highway system in the 1950s. The interstate, while it ushered in an era of great prosperity, has also been blamed for the decline of the cities and the loss of services to poor and minority communities. Many advocates fear that a poorly designed information superhighway could lead to further marginalization of the underprivileged in society.

The big telecommunications players are at pains to promise this won't happen, and both Pacific Telesis and AT&T-McCaw have signed commitments with community groups in California to ensure that the state's minority, low-income, inner-city, and disabled populations are wired into the electronic future. But a recent study of early plans for advanced communications networks by a coalition of groups (including the National Association for the Advancement of Colored People, the Consumer Federation of America, and the Center for Media Education) suggests that poor and minority neighborhoods are already becoming victims of "electronic redlining."

"Everyone is going to need affordable access to interactive communications services to ensure that the public has access to a basic range of information," explains Jeffrey Chester. He says it's conceivable that the media could evolve so that C-SPAN is the only source of information for what's going on in Congress, making a lower-cost tier of information services vital for democracy.

"We don't know what a Twenty-first Century version of public television will look like, but we can start thinking about it when we look at the Internet and freenet and community radio stations," he suggests.

Freenets, for example, provide access to e-mail, computer databases, and the Internet in such cities as Buffalo, Cleveland, and Seattle, through libraries and other outreach programs. "Those services are not going to become a part of the information superhighway without a real public policy to ensure that they are a viable—not marginal—part of the media system," warns Chester.

Another access question raised by the information economy is that when information is bought and sold in units, you can only know as much as you can afford. The commercial databases used by large corporations, law firms, and news services are

"The interstate...has been blamed for the decline of the cities and the loss of services to poor and minority communities."

expensive. In legal cases, in particular, this puts the well-heeled at a distinct advantage. Most of the material in legal databases consists of case law and judicial decisions in the public domain, but such companies as West Publishing maintain that they own the copyright for the page numbers of the decisions, giving them an effective monopoly in the legal database market for many states and Federal courts. Furthermore, local, state, and federal Governments maintain many valuable databases which are not currently accessible to their putative owners—the general public.

While this is a dark rendering of tomorrow, the future of cyberspace could be a lot more promising. Activists worldwide are already using advanced computer networks to share information and coordinate strategies. And citizens across the country could instantaneously gather information from a variety of sources uncensored by the corporate media.

"The U.S. Customs Service is currently investigating how PGP was exported."

But the perils of the Information Age are broad. In his book, *The Cult of Information*, Theodore Roszak reminds us that information cannot replace—and may even obscure—knowledge, insight, and wisdom. "Every mature technology brings an immediate gain followed by enormous long-term liabilities," he writes. "How things will balance out is a matter of vigilance, moral courage, and the distribution of power."

Consider the story of Philip Zimmermann, a software engineer who believes in "freeware"—software given away to help people better use their computers. In 1991, Zimmermann released an encryption program called Pretty Good Privacy (PGP) to help protect electronic mail; since then it has spread all over the world. On the day that Boris Yeltsin went to war against his own parliament, Zimmermann received an e-mail message from Latvia: "Phil I wish you to know: Let it never be, but if dictatorship takes over Russia your PGP is widespread from Baltic to Far East now and will help democratic people if necessary. Thanks." But despite the worldwide availability of PGP and other encryption tools, this technology is still controlled by national-security interests. The U.S. Customs Service is currently investigating how PGP was exported.

Testifying last year before the House Subcommittee for Economic Policy, Trade, and the Environment, Zimmermann worried that "some elements of the Government" were intent on denying citizens their privacy. "This is unsettling because in a democracy, it is possible for bad people to occasionally get elected—sometimes very bad people," said Zimmermann.

"Normally, a well-functioning democracy has ways to remove these people from power. But the wrong technology infrastructure could allow such a future government to watch every move anyone makes to oppose it. It could very well be the last government we ever elect."

Resolving the Encryption Dilemma: The Case for "Clipper"[3]

THE U.S. GOVERNMENT HAS LAUNCHED A PROGRAM TO EXPAND SECURITY AND PRIVACY PROTECTION FOR ELECTRONIC COMMUNICATIONS WHILE PRESERVING THE GOVERNMENT'S ABILITY TO CONDUCT AUTHORIZED WIRETAPS. DESPITE ATTACKS FROM CIVIL LIBERTARIANS, THE APPROACH IS THE BEST WAY TO BALANCE INDIVIDUAL PRIVACY WITH THE SOCIAL GOOD.

"As individuals and companies swarm onto the Internet, they are also beginning to encrypt electronic mail and computer files."

IMAGINE you are the program manager for a new, energy-efficient airplane. You fax the design plans to the manager of an overseas plant that will manufacture parts of the plane. You also discuss the design by phone with engineers in the plant. A few months later, your company loses a bid for a fleet of planes to an overseas competitor who proposed a nearly identical design. The rival stole your plans by intercepting your voice and fax communications. Fortunately, electronic communication can be protected against such industrial espionage with encryption—scrambling of data in such a manner that they are unintelligible to anyone other than the intended receiver. In today's digital world, communications are first converted into ones and zeroes. An encryption algorithm mathematically transforms these bits into a stream of digits that seems random. Performing the transformation requires a secret key—which is also a random-seeming string of ones and zeroes; the receiver uses this key to decrypt and recover the original message. The more digits there are in this key, the more secure the protection; each additional bit doubles the number of possible combinations that a would be snooper must try.

Encryption has been used in the United States primarily to protect classified state and military secrets from foreign governments. However, its use outside the government has been steadily increasing ever since the Data Encryption Standard (DES) was adopted as a federal standard in 1977. DES, which is based on a 56-bit key, is now used extensively by the banking industry to protect money transfers and by some corporations to protect sensitive communications transmitted through company networks or the telephone system. As individuals and companies swarm onto the Internet, they are also beginning to encrypt electronic mail and computer files.

---

[3] Article by Dorothy Elizabeth Robling Denning, professor of computer science at Georgetown University and a specialist in computer and communication security, also the author of *Cryptography and Data Security*, from *Technology Review* 98:48-55 Jl '95. Copyright © 1995 *Technology Review*. Reprinted with permission.

But encryption is a dual-edged sword. The spread of high-quality encryption could undermine the value of wiretaps—a technology that has helped ensnare organized crime figures and other menaces to society. With the government essentially locked out, computers and telecommunications systems would become safe havens for outlaws and terrorists. In one recent child pornography case in California, evidence was concealed in encrypted computer files that could not be broken.

Encryption also could interfere with U.S. intelligence abroad, because it could allow a country like Iraq to operate behind a wall of electronic secrecy. Encryption technology is therefore subject to export controls: products that incorporate DES or other strong encryption methods cannot generally be exported. This has been a sore point with U.S. industry, which has argued that since DES-based products are manufactured overseas also, the controls have succeeded only in putting U.S. industry at a disadvantage. However, even though export controls have not prevented DES and other methods of encryption from being implemented elsewhere, the controls have protected valuable and fragile intelligence capabilities.

Encryption poses a threat to organizations and individuals, too. For effective secrecy, a minimal number of people should be allowed to know the encryption key. This practice invites disaster, though, as valuable information stored in encrypted files could become inaccessible if the key were accidentally lost or corrupted, intentionally destroyed, or maybe even held for ransom by a disgruntled employee or former employee. Encryption also could enable an employee to transmit corporate secrets to a competitor or to cover up fraud, embezzlement, and other illegal activity.

Despite such problems, almost everyone agrees that individuals and organizations need access to encryption technology. With the spread of computer networks, people are conducting more and more of their personal and business affairs through computer and telephone networks. Encryption is essential for erecting a wall of privacy around those communications.

To resolve the encryption dilemma, the Clinton administration in 1993 proposed a new approach, called "key-escrow" encryption. The idea is to make broadly available an essentially unbreakable encryption scheme. The catch: to allow for emergency access to information, the keys to unlock the keys to unlock the encrypted data would be held by the U.S. government.

The idea is to allow the most secure encryption, but with a built-in emergency decryption capability that allows authorized officials, with the cooperation of one or more trusted parties who hold keys, to decrypt data. The initial embodiment of this system is a microelectronic device called the Clipper chip, and its escrow agents are the National Institute of Standards and Technology (NIST) and the Department of Treasury's Automated Systems

Division. In principle, commercial organizations also could serve as escrow agents.

The Clipper chip uses an encryption algorithm called Skipjack and keys of 80 bits—24 bits longer than DES keys. The extra 24 bits provides 2^{24} or about 16 million times the security against trial-and-error guesses at keys. The Skipjack algorithm was designed by the National Security Agency (NSA) and is classified.

Some civil libertarians have adamantly opposed this plan, worrying that the key escrow system will put the communications of honest persons needlessly at risk. After all, they argue, criminals are not going to be dumb enough to use an encryption scheme to which the government holds the keys. The logical next step, they say, would be to outlaw other methods of encryption, striking a blow at citizens' right to communicate away from the government's eyes and ears. Thus, critics argue, Clipper heralds future erosions in privacy rights—Big Brother on a chip.

Actually, Clipper represents a more secure approach to encryption than the two other avenues that the government has considered. One approach would use an encryption method with short enough keys that it becomes practical for any eavesdropper to guess a key by trying all possibilities. The other would use long keys, but have a built-in "trapdoor" allowing someone familiar with the system to find the key. The problem with this approach is that someone else might discover the trapdoor. Clipper avoids these weaker methods, offering a high-security solution to the encryption dilemma.

"The logical next step, they say, would be to outlaw other methods of encryption, striking a blow at citizens' right to communicate...."

Holding Keys in Escrow

The specifications for Clipper were adopted last year as the Escrowed Encryption Standard for use with sensitive but unclassified telephone communications, including voice, fax, and data. The EES standard is voluntary; nongovernment agencies have no obligation to use it, and government agencies can choose between it and any other encryption standard, such as DES. With the U.S. government holding the keys, EES poses no threat to foreign intelligence operations and thus EES-based encryption products can be exported.

The first product to use the Clipper chip is a device that plugs into a standard phone between the handset and the base unit. Manufactured by AT&T, the device can encrypt any conversation as long as the party at the other end has a compatible device. After a call is established in the usual way, one party presses a button on the device to activate its "secure mode." The two devices then enter into a digital, behind-the-scenes conversation to establish a "session key" that is unique to the conversation. Each device passes this 80-bit session key to its Clipper chip; the Clipper uses this key to encrypt outgoing communications and decrypt incoming communications. Before encrypting any data, however, the chip computes and transmits a string of bits called the law enforcement access field (LEAF). The LEAF contains the session key for the conversation and is what enables authorized government officials to decrypt the data.

To protect the session key in the LEAF, it is itself encrypted. Each Clipper chip has a unique identifier (ID) and associated "device-unique key." The device-unique key is split into two components, each of which is given to a separate escrow agent. Using this device-unique key, the Clipper chip encrypts the session key. The encrypted session key is then put into the LEAF along with the chip ID. The entire LEAF is further encrypted under a common "family key" so that even the chip ID is not transmitted in the clear. These two layers of encryption provide a strong shield against an eavesdropper learning the session key and then decrypting the data.

Users of Clipper don't need to be aware of any of these details; they simply use their phones as always. The complexity surfaces when a law enforcement official encounters encrypted communications on a tapped phone line. First, the communications must be passed through a special device, known as a decrypt processor, to ascertain if they are Clipper communications. If they are, the processor locates and decrypts the LEAF, and then extracts the chip ID. (Because the same session key is used to encrypt both ends of the conversation, it is not necessary to obtain the chip ID for both parties.)

But knowledge of this chip ID alone will not allow the wiretap to be deciphered. What is needed are the two components of the device-unique key associated with this ID—and this information is what is held by the two key escrow agents. So the law enforcement officials, having obtained this ID, must request these components from the escrow agents. These key components are then entered into the decrypt processor, which combines them to form the device-unique key. This device-unique key, in turn, is used to decrypt the session key in the LEAF. Knowledge of this session key enables the conversation to be decrypted. If subsequent conversations on the intercepted line are encrypted, the decrypt processor can decrypt the session key directly, without going through the two escrow agents. This allows for real-time decryption.

Safeguards

Critics maintain that the very idea of a key escrow system raises the risk that encrypted messages will be decoded by the wrong people. Without proper safeguards, an intruder might break into a computer containing escrowed keys, download the keys, and use the keys to decrypt communications intercepted illegally. Alternatively, a corrupt employee of an escrow agent might use the keys to engage in illegal wiretapping or sell the keys to a foreign government or to the mafia.

Clipper's key escrow system is being developed with extensive controls to protect against such threats. One fundamental safeguard is key secrecy. Keys and key components are generated in computers and are never displayed or printed out in forms readable by humans. In addition, they are always stored and transmitted in encrypted form.

Physical security is used extensively to protect sensitive material. The computer workstations at NIST and the Department of Treasury that are used for key escrow functions are used for nothing else and are kept in secured facilities. The chips are programmed with their IDs and device-unique keys in a vault designed for handling classified information.

As the Clipper system develops, keys are stored on floppy disks in double-locked safes and carried manually, wrapped in tamper-detecting packages, from the facility where the chips are programmed to the escrow agents and from the escrow agents to the law enforcement facility that is tapping the call. Ultimately, the keys will be transmitted electronically—in encrypted form— between the chip-programming facility and escrowagent workstations, and between those workstations and the law-enforcement decrypt processors. Separation of duties limits the power of a single person or agency. Different organizations operate the chip-programming facility (so far, Mykotronx Inc. of Torrance, Calif., runs the only one), the key escrow services (NIST and the Department of the Treasury), and the decrypt processors (law enforcement agencies). Escrow officers are not allowed to program the chips, operate a decrypt processor, or even have a decrypt processor in their possession. Law-enforcement officers have access to a decrypt processor but not to keys (keys cannot be extracted from a decrypt processor). Escrow officers will attach a "self-destruct" date, corresponding to the end of the period of authorized surveillance, to keys transmitted to a decrypt processor. This measure precludes the use of keys after a wiretap order expires.

> *"Escrow officers are not allowed to program the chips, operate a decrypt processor, or even have a decrypt processor in their possession."*

To limit the power of a single individual to abuse the system, the key escrow system requires that at least two people be present whenever a critical function is performed or when sensitive data might be exposed. In fact, because each chip's device-unique key is split into two components, and each component is held by a separate key escrow agent, it is not possible for one person to act independently. Neither component by itself reveals any information about the key; to reconstruct and use the key, both escrow agents must supply their parts. Further, within each escrow agency, it takes two escrow officers to unlock the safes that contain the key components. Similar two-person control systems have worked successfully in the military to control nuclear-launch codes and in the banking world.

Detailed procedures govern all operations that involve escrowed keys, including generation of the keys, programming of the chips, storage and release of escrowed keys, and government decryption. For example, a request for escrowed key components must include certification that the official is authorized to conduct the wiretap (normally established by a court order). All operations that involve the generation, release, or use of escrowed keys are logged. From the logs, it should be possible to determine that keys are used only as authorized, and only to decrypt communications intercepted during a period of authorized surveillance.

The key escrow system is undergoing independent validation and verification. In addition to paid contractors, four individuals, including myself, have been voluntarily reviewing the system as an extension of our earlier review of the Skipjack algorithm, on which Clipper is based. Based on what I have seen so far of the design, I conclude that there is no significant risk of an insider or outsider acquiring unauthorized access to keys.

"The only way to make sure that an algorithm is any good is to let many people analyze it and try to crack it...."

As the Clipper system proves to be strong and resistant to abuse, the technology will, I believe, become more widely accepted. The Department of Defense already uses Capstone—a more advanced chip that is built into a PC card named Fortezze—to provide security for electronic mail. Fortezza offers an attractive option for secure electronic commerce: it contains a mechanism for electronically "signing" a digital document so that the recipient can verify the sender's identity. The American National Standards Institute (ANSI) is developing banking standards that could use Fortezza technology.

Who Do You Trust?

These safeguards have not eased everyone's mind. One big concern is that the Skipjack encryption algorithm on which Clipper is based is classified. Because Skipjack is not open to public review, some people have questioned whether NSA might have intentionally sabotaged the algorithm with a trapdoor that would allow the government to decode encrypted communications while bypassing the escrow agents.

Critics also worry that this secret algorithm might harbor a design flaw that would leave it vulnerable to cracking. Such concerns have a legitimate base. Designing strong encryption algorithms is a difficult task. The only way to make sure that an algorithm is any good is to let many people analyze it and try to crack it over an extended period of time; many encryption schemes that appeared strong when first proposed later succumbed to attack.

A noteworthy example is the RSA algorithm, named after Ronald Rivest, Adi Shamir, and Len Adleman, all of whom were at MIT when they invented it in 1977. Breaking RSA requires the solution of a difficult mathematical problem: given a large number, what are the prime numbers that must be multiplied together to yield that number? A very simple example, with a low number, would be to find the prime factors of 1,261; a few minutes with a pocket calculator, or a trivial computer program, will reveal the answer: 13 and 97. But as the number to be factored increases in length, this task seems to get exponentially more difficult. When the algorithm was first introduced, Rivest predicted that it would take a quadrillion years to factor a 125-digit number using the fastest factoring methods then known. But factoring methods have advanced rapidly, and in 1994 a 129-digit number was factored in 8 months through the use of some 1,600 computers scattered around the world. RSA still appears to be very strong for numbers that are 200 digits or more.

To address the concerns about weaknesses and trapdoors in Skipjack, the government invited outside experts to independently review the algorithm and report their findings. I participated in that review along with four other cryptographers in 1993. We examined NSA's internal design and evaluation of Skipjack and found them to be the same as used with algorithms that protect the country's most sensitive classified information. Skipjack underwent thorough evaluation over many years following its initial design in 1987, and the specific structures used in the algorithm have an even longer history of intense study. We also conducted some analysis and experiments of our own to determine if the algorithm had any properties that might make it susceptible to attack. Based on our analysis and experiments, we concluded that there was no significant risk that Skipjack contained a trapdoor or could be broken.

"Agreements might be reached that would allow some other governments to hold the keys or have access to the classified technology...."

Although publication of Skipjack would enable more people to confirm its strength, NSA is unlikely to do so; declassifying Skipjack would benefit foreign adversaries and allow the algorithm to be used without the key escrow features. Even if Skipjack were made public, it would probably be years before skeptics would accept its strength. When DES was introduced in 1975, it was similarly distrusted because of some NSA involvement even though the algorithm was developed by IBM and made public.

Still, Clipper's use of a classified algorithm does limit its acceptability. There are many people who will never trust the NSA; for them, Clipper is tainted goods. In addition, many potential foreign buyers will not accept a classified algorithm or keys held by the U.S. government, although Mykotronx has reported that some potential foreign buyers are not concerned about these factors. Agreements might be reached that would allow some other governments to hold the keys or have access to the classified technology, but such agreements would likely be limited to a few countries.

Moreover, as long as the algorithm is supposed to remain secret, it must be implemented in tamper-resistant hardware. That's because there is no known way of hiding classified information in software. This precludes software implementations, which are generally cheaper. On the other hand, hardware generally provides greater security for keys and greater integrity for the algorithms than software, so some customers will want hardware products.

Although key escrow is voluntary, critics say that the introduction of Clipper points national policy in a disturbing direction. The main premise here is that the criminals that Clipper is meant to uncover would be unlikely to choose an encryption scheme to which the U.S. government holds the keys. Many forms of une-scrowed encryption are already on the market, and more are being developed. One file encryption package, called Pretty Good Privacy (PGP), is spreading as free software through the Internet and becoming popular for encrypting e-mail. Unescrowed encryption with time-tested algorithms such as DES and RSA is also being integrated into commercial products. The only way to accomplish the goals of Clipper, skeptics therefore maintain, would be to ban unescrowed encryption systems—a prospect that enrages some defenders of electronic privacy.

But it is not self-evident that criminals will shun Clipper. Whether they use the escrowed encryption system will depend in part on what else is available—and in particular what other forms of encryption are built into the most widely used commercial products. While PGP has a certain grassroots appeal, many organizations will be reluctant to trust their assets to software obtained over the Internet.

"Vendors might favor key escrow because they will be able to build it into products that are exported."

Over time, market forces could easily favor escrowed encryption. Some organizations might choose to use Clipper because the high quality of its encryption outweighs the slight risk that information will fall into the wrong hands. Vendors might favor key escrow because they will be able to build it into products that are exported. And the government's adoption of escrowed encryption will set a de facto standard; any company that needs to exchange encrypted information with federal agencies will need to use compatible encryption. If escrowed encryption becomes a business standard, many criminals will tend to use it—the convenience will outweigh the risk.

Even if criminals do not use Clipper, the government's voluntary initiative serves a useful purpose. If the government instead promoted strong encryption without key escrow, this would accelerate the spread of encryption that the government could not decrypt and the use of such encryption by criminals. The government decided that it would not be responsible to use its own expertise and resources to pursue encryption standards that fundamentally subvert law enforcement and threaten public safety and national security.

Escrow Alternatives

The basic concept of key escrow does not necessarily depend on handing the keys to government agencies. Private-sector organizations—licensed and bonded—could serve as key escrow agents instead. Although nongovernment escrow agents are unlikely to provide any greater protection than government ones operating under the controls stipulated for the Clipper system, they could be more widely accepted by those who are particularly concerned about government abuse. In addition, commercial escrow agents could make their services available to the private sector so that individuals and organizations could acquire their own keys for data recovery purposes. Clipper's key escrow system does not have this capability

Some encryption products already have private key escrow capabilities whereby an organization can escrow its own keys. In addition, several companies and individuals have proposed commercial key escrow approaches, with third party agents. Some of these proposals, for example, one from Trusted Information Systems of Glenwood, Md., use software with unclassified algorithms. Commercial key escrow might achieve greater acceptability than Clipper and encourage the adoption of key escrow over unescrowed encryption. For that reason, the government has been working with industry to find alternatives to Clipper that might better meet the needs of industry and users.

For commercial key escrow to work, legislation may be required to deal with issues relating to liability and jurisdiction. What happens, for instance, if a state or local law enforcement agency needs keys held by an escrow agent located in another state? Normally, a warrant cannot be taken across state boundaries except during federal investigations.

Another important question surrounding commercial key escrow is whether such systems will be exportable. Companies that make encryption products would like to be able to manufacture a single product line for both domestic and international sales. Moreover, the opening of an export market would help expand the market for key escrow encryption—indirectly, at least, lowering the chances that criminals will use unescrowed encryption. So far, the U.S. government has not said whether it would permit the export of commercial key escrow or software-based systems. At issue is whether the government is assured that it will have a way to decrypt information when it deems it necessary to do so.

An exportable encryption scheme would also facilitate an international encryption standard—an important goal, given that organizations often need to communicate securely with customers, suppliers, and partners outside the United States. So far, no international encryption standard provides end-to-end protection of confidentiality. DES is used worldwide, especially by the financial industry, but mainly for authenticating financial transactions rather than shrouding messages in secrecy. Many countries around the world have adopted a system called Global System for Mobile to keep mobile radio communications secure. But GSM encrypts only the over-the-air link between a mobile phone and a base station. Communications that travel through wires and cables therefore remain vulnerable to interception.

Key escrow encryption offers the best hope for an international standard that would facilitate such international communications. In fact, an encryption method that does not provide a capability for government access is unlikely to be accepted as an international standard; other countries share the U.S. desire not to be left in the electronic lurch. Each country could designate its own escrow agents, which could be either government or commercial organizations. Users might have the option of choosing an escrow agent from this list. Bankers Trust has outlined a proposal for just such an approach. Like Clipper, the Bankers Trust system would use hardware for its greater security; unlike Clipper, however, the algorithm would be unclassified and therefore more suitable for commercial and international use.

Will Clipper Catch On?

Much opposition to Clipper stems from the belief that the government has an insatiable and unsavory desire to gather information about its law-abiding citizens. Clipper, say critics, is a bad idea because it permits such activity. Despite the system's safeguards, some people are concerned that a future administration or corrupt police officer could obtain keys to conduct questionable if not outright illegal wiretaps.

"The Fourth Amendment specifically protects against unreasonable searches and seizures...."

At a forum held at MIT last September, professor Rivest argued that the fundamental question Clipper raises is: Should American citizens have the right to have communications and records that the government cannot access even when properly authorized? A case can be made that from a constitutional standpoint, no such absolute right exists. The Fourth Amendment specifically protects against unreasonable searches and seizures while allowing those conducted with a court order.

While abuse of the Clipper system cannot be ruled out, it is unlikely. Neither the public nor Congress has tolerated such activity in the past, and federal wiretap laws, government regulations and procedures, and congressional committees have been established to protect against their occurrence in the future. Wiretaps are conducted under tight controls and subject to considerable oversight. Clipper includes an additional layer of protection since anyone wishing to conduct a wiretap must also acquire a special decrypt processor and keys from the escrow agents.

The opposition to Clipper makes its widespread adoption by no means assured. But escrowed encryption offers the best hope for reaping the benefits of encryption while minimizing its potential harm. Rejection of key escrow would have profound implications for criminal justice. As computer networks continue to expand into every area of society and commerce, court-ordered wiretaps and seizures of records could become tools of the past, and the information superhighway a safe haven for criminal activity.

Battle of the Clipper Chip[4]

On a sunny spring day in Mountain View, Calif., 50 angry activists are plotting against the United States Government. They may not look subversive sitting around a conference table dressed in T-shirts and jeans and eating burritos, but they are self-proclaimed saboteurs. They are the Cypherpunks, a loose confederation of computer hackers, hardware engineers and high-tech rabble-rousers.

The precise object of their rage is the Clipper chip, officially known as the MYK-78 and not much bigger than a tooth. Just another tiny square of plastic covering a silicon thicket. A computer chip, from the outside indistinguishable from thousands of others. It seems improbable that this black Chiclet is the focal point of a battle that may determine the degree to which our civil liberties survive in the next century. But that is the shared belief in this room.

The Clipper chip has prompted what might be considered the first holy war of the information highway. Two weeks ago, the war got bloodier, as a researcher circulated a report that the chip might have a serious technical flaw. But at its heart, the issue is political, not technical. The Cypherpunks consider the Clipper the lever that Big Brother is using to pry into the conversations, messages and transactions of the computer age. These high-tech Paul Reveres are trying to mobilize America against the evil portent of a "cyberspace police state" as one of their Internet jeremiads put it. Joining them in the battle is a formidable force, including almost all of the communications and computer industries, many members of Congress and political columnists of all stripes. The anti-Clipper aggregation is an equal-opportunity club, uniting the American Civil Liberties Union and Rush Limbaugh.

The Clipper's defenders, who are largely in the Government, believe it represents the last chance to protect personal safety and national security against a developing information anarchy that fosters criminals, terrorists and foreign foes. Its adherents pose it as the answer, or at least part of the answer, to a problem created by an increasingly sophisticated application of an age-old technology: cryptography, the use of secret codes.

For centuries, cryptography was the domain of armies and diplomatic corps. Now it has a second purpose: protecting personal and corporate privacy. Computer technology and advanced telecommunications equipment have drawn precious business information and intimate personal communications out into the open. This phenomenon is well known to the current Prince of

---

4 Article by Steven Levy, from *The New York Times Magazine* Jl 3, '94 6:4. Copyright © 1994 Steven Levy. Reprinted with permission of Sterling Lord Literistic, Inc.

Wales, whose intimate cellular phone conversations were intercepted, recorded and broadcast worldwide. And corporations realize that competitors can easily intercept their telephone conversations, electronic messages and faxes. High tech has created a huge privacy gap. But miraculously, a fix has emerged: cheap, easy-to-use, virtually unbreakable encryption. Cryptography is the silver bullet by which we can hope to reclaim our privacy.

The solution, however, has one drawback: cryptography shields the law abiding and the lawless equally. Law-enforcement and intelligence agencies contend that if strong codes are widely available, their efforts to protect the public would be paralyzed. So they have come up with a compromise, a way to neutralize such encryption. That's the Clipper chip and that compromise is what the war is about.

"A potential eaves-dropper has no key and therefore cannot understand the conversation or read the data transmission."

The idea is to give the Government means to override other people"s codes, according to a concept called "key escrow." Employing normal cryptography, two parties can communicate in total privacy, with both of them using a digital "key" to encrypt and decipher the conversation or message. A potential eavesdropper has no key and therefore cannot understand the conversation or read the data transmission. But with Clipper, an additional key—created at the time the equipment is manufactured—is held by the Government in escrow. With a court-approved wiretap, an agency like the F.B.I. could listen in. By adding Clipper chips to telephones, we could have a system that assures communications will be private—from everybody but the Government.

And that's what rankles Clipper's many critics. Why, they ask, should people accused of no crime have to give Government the keys to their private communications? Why shouldn't the market rather than Government determine what sort of cryptosystem wins favor. And isn't it true that the use of key escrow will make our technology so unattractive to the international marketplace that the United States will lose its edge in the lucrative telecommunications and computer fields? Clipper might clip the entire economy.

Nonetheless, on Feb. 4 the White House announced its approval of the Clipper chip, which had been under study as a Government standard since last April, and the Crypto War broke out in full force. Within a month, one civil liberties group, Computer Professionals for Social Responsibility, received 47,000 electronic missives urging a stop to Clipper. "The war is upon us," wrote Tim May, co-founder of the Cypherpunks, in an urgent electronic dispatch soon after the announcement. "Clinton and Gore folks have shown themselves to be enthusiastic supporters of Big Brother."

And though the Clinton Administration's endorsement of Clipper as a Government standard required no Congressional approval, rumblings of discontent came from both sides of the Capitol. Senator Patrick J. Leahy, the Vermont Democrat whose subcomittee has held contentious hearings on the matter, has called the plan a "misstep," charging that "the Government should not be in the business of mandating particular technologies."

Two weeks ago, an AT&T Bell Laboratories researcher revealed that he had found a serious flaw in the Clipper technology itself, enabling techno-savvy lawbreakers to bypass the security fuction of the chip in some applications. Besides being a bad idea, Clipper's foes now say, it doesn't even work properly.

Yet the defenders of Clipper have refused to back down, claiming that the scheme—which is, they often note, voluntary—is an essential means of stemming an increasing threat to public safety and security by strong encryption in everyday use. Even if Clipper itself has to go back to the drawing board, its Government designers will come up with something quite similar. The underlying issue remains unchanged: If something like Clipper is not implemented, writes Dorothy E. Denning, a Georgetown University computer scientist, "All communications on the information highway would be immune from lawful interception. In a world threatened by international organized crime, terrorism and rogue governments, this would be folly."

The claims from both sides sound wild, almost apocalyptic. The passion blurs the problem: Can we protect our privacy in an age of computers—without also protecting the dark forces in society?

The crypto war is the inevitable consequence of a remarkable discovery made almost 20 years ago, a breakthrough that combined with the microelectronics revolution to thrust the once-obscure field of cryptography into the mainstream of communications policy.

It began with Whitfield Diffie, a young computer scientist and cryptographer. He did not work for the Government, which was strange because in the 1960's almost all serious crypto in this country was done under Federal auspices, specifically at the Fort Meade, Md., headquarters of the supersecret National Security Agency. Though it became bigger than the C.I.A., the N.S.A. was for years unknown to Americans; the Washington Beltway joke was that the initials stood for "No Such Agency." Its working premise has always been that no information about its activities should ever be revealed. Its main mission involved cryptography, and the security agency so dominated the field that it had the power to rein in even those few experts in the field who were not on its payroll.

But Whitfield Diffie never got that message. He had been bitten by the cryptography bug at age 10 when his father, a professor, brought home the entire crypto shelf of the City College library in New York. Then he lost interest, until he arrived at M.I.T.'s Artifical Intelligence Laboratory in 1966. Two things rekindled his passion. Now trained as a mathematician, he had an affinity for the particular challenges of sophisticated crypto. Just as important, he says, "I was always concerned about individuals, an individual's privacy as opposed to Goverment secrecy."

Diffie, now 50, is still committed to those beliefs. When asked about his politics, he says, "I like to describe myself as an iconoclast." He is a computer security specialist for Sun Microsystems, a celebrated cryptographer and an experienced hand at Congressional testimony. But he looks like he stumbled out of a Tom Robbins novel—with blond hair that falls to his shoulders and a longish beard that seems a virtual trademark among code makers. At a Palo Alto, Calif., coffeehouse one morning, he describes, in clipped, precise cadence, how he and Martin E. Hellman, an electrical engineering professor at Stanford University, created a crypto revolution.

Diffie was dissatisfied with the security on a new time-sharing computer system being developed by M.I.T. in the 1960's. Files would be protected by passwords, but he felt that was insufficient. The system had a generic flaw. A system manager had access to all passwords. "If a subpeona was served against the system managers, they would sell you out, because they had no interest in going to jail," Diffie says. A perfect system would eliminate the need for a trusted third party.

This led Diffie to think about a more general problem in cryptography: key management. Even before Julius Caesar devised a simple cipher to encode his military messages, cryptography worked by means of keys. That is, an original message (what is now called "plaintext") was encrypted by the sender into seeming gibberish (known as "ciphertext"). The receiver, using the same key, decrypted the message back into the original plaintext. For instance, the Caesar key was the simple replacement of each letter by the letter three places down in the alphabet. If you knew the key, you could encrypt the word help into the nonsense word khos; the recipient of the message would decrypt the message back to help.

The problem came with protecting the key. Since anyone who knew the Caesar key would be able to understand the encoded message, it behooved the Romans to change that key as often as possible. But if you change the key, how do you inform your spies behind enemy lines? (If you tell them using the old code, which may have already been cracked, your enemies will then learn the new code.) For centuries, generals and diplomats have faced that predicament. But a few years ago, it took on added urgency.

With computers and advanced telecommunications, customers outside Government were discovering a need for information security. Cryptography was the answer, but how could it be applied widely, considering the problem of keys? The best answer to date was something called a key-management repository, where two parties who wanted secrecy would go to a trusted third party who would generate a new key for the private session. But that required just what Diffie deplored—an unwanted third wheel.

"The virtue of cryptography should be that you don't have to trust anybody not directly involved with your communication," Diffie says. "Without conventional key distribution centers, which involved trusting third parties, I couldn't figure how you could build a system to secure, for instance, all the phones in the country."

When Diffie moved to Stanford University in 1969, he foresaw the rise of home computer terminals and began pondering the problem of how to use them to make transactions. "I got to thinking how you could possibly have electronic business, because signed letters of intent, contracts and all seemed so critical," he says. He devoured what literature he could find outside the National Security Agency. And in the mid-1970's, Diffie and Hellman achieved a stunning breakthrough that changed cryptography forever. They split the cryptographic key.

In their system, every user has two keys, a public one and a private one, that are unique to their owner. Whatever is scrambled by one key can be unscrambled by the other. It works like this: If I want to send a message to Whit Diffie, I first obtain his public key. (For complicated mathematical reasons, it is possible to distribute one's public key freely without compromising security; a potential enemy will have no advantage in code-cracking if he holds your public key alone.) Then I use that key to encode the message. Now it's gobbledygook and only one person in the world can decode it—Whit Diffie, who holds the other, private, key. If he wants to respond to me with a secret message, he uses my public key to encode his answer. And I decode it, using my private key.

It was an amazing solution, but even more remarkable was that this split-key system solved both of Diffie's problems, the desire to shield communications from eavesdroppers and also to provide a secure electronic identification for contracts and financial transactions done by computer. It provided the identification by the use of "digital signatures" that verify the sender much the same way that a real signature validates a check or contract.

Suddenly, the ancient limitations on cryptography had vanished. Now, perhaps before the millennium, strong cryptography could find its way to every telephone, computer and fax machine—if users wanted it. Subsequent variations on the Diffie-Hellman scheme focused on using crypto algorithms to insure the anonymity of transactions. Using these advances, it is now possible to think of replacing money with digital cash—while maintaining the comforting untraceability of bills and coins. The dark art of cryptography has become a tool of liberation.

From the moment Diffie and Hellman published their findings in 1976, the National Security Agency's crypto monopoly was effectively terminated. In short order, three M.I.T. mathematicians—Ronald L. Rivest, Adi Shamir and Leonard M. Adleman—developed a system with which to put the Diffie and Hellman findings into practice. It was known by their initials, RSA. It seemed capable of creating codes that even the N.S.A. could not

"...it is now possible to think of replacing money with digital cash...."

break. They formed a company to sell their new system; it was only a matter of time before thousands and then millions of people began using strong encryption.

That was the National Security Agency's greatest nightmare. Every company, every citizen now had routine access to the sorts of cryptographic technology that not many years ago ranked alongside the atom bomb as a source of power. Every call, every computer message, every fax in the world could be harder to decipher than the famous German "Enigma" machine of World War II. Maybe even impossible to decipher!

The genie was out of the bottle. Next question: Could the genie be made to wear a leash and collar? Enter the Clipper chip.

When illustrating the Government's need to control crypto, Jim Kallstrom, the agent in charge of the special operations division of the New York office of the F.B.I., quickly shifts the discussion to the personal: "Are you married? Do you have a child? O.K., someone kidnaps one of your kids and they are holding your kid in this fortress up in the Bronx. Now, we have probable cause that your child is inside this fortress. We have a search warrant. But for some reason, we cannot get in there. They made it out of some new metal, or something, right? Nothing'll cut it, right? And there are guys in there, laughing at us. That's what the basis of this issue really is—we've got a situation now where a technology has become so sophisticated that the whole notion of a legal process is at stake here!"

"Wiretapping is among law enforcement's most cherished weapons."

Kallstrom is a former head of the Bureau Tech Squad, involved in the bugging operation that brought John Gotti to justice. Some have described him as the F.B.I.'s answer to "Q," the gadget wizard of the James Bond tales.

"From the standpoint of law enforcement, there's a superbig threat out there—this guy is gonna build this domain in the Bronx now, because he's got a new steel door and none of the welding torches, none of the boomerangs, nothing we have is gonna blast our way in there. Sure, we want those new steel doors ourselves, to protect our banks, to protect the American corporation trade secrets, patent rights, technology. But people operating in legitimate business are not violating the laws—it becomes a different ball of wax when we have probable cause and we have to get into that domain. Do we want a digital superhighway where not only the commerce of the nation can take place but where major criminals can operate impervious to the legal process? If we don't want that, then we have to look at Clipper."

Wiretapping is among law enforcement's most cherished weapons. Only 919 Federal, state and local taps were authorized last year, but police agencies consider them essential to fighting crime. Obviously if criminals communicate using military-grade cryptosystems, wiretapping them becomes impossible.

For two years, the F.B.I. has been urging Congress to pass the proposed Digital Telephony and Communications Privacy Act, which would in essence require that new communications technologies be designed to facilitate wiretapping. Even if the bill should somehow pass, overcoming the opposition of the communications industry and civil libertarians, the extra effort and expense will be wasted if the only thing the wiretappers can hear is the hissy white noise of encrypted phone conversations and faxes. If cryptography is not controlled, wiretapping could be rendered obsolete. Louis J. Freeh, the Director of the F.B.I., surely fears that prospect. He has told Congress that preserving the ability to intercept communications legally, in the face of these technological advances, is "the No. 1 law enforcement, public safety and national security issue facing us today."

Some people criticize Clipper on the basis that truly sophisticated criminals would never use it, preferring other easily obtained systems that use high-grade cryptography. Despite Clipper, kidnappers and drug kingpins may construct Kallstrom's virtual fort in the Bronx with impunity, laughing at potential wiretappers.

The Government understands the impossibility of eradicating strong crypto. Its objective is instead to prevent unbreakable encryption from becoming routine. If that happens, even the stupidest criminal would be liberated from the threat of surveillance. But by making Clipper the standard, the Government is betting that only a tiny percentage of users would use other encryption or try to defeat the Clipper.

At a rare public appearance in March at a conference on computers and privacy, Stewart A. Baker, then general counsel of the National Security Agency, tried to explain. "The concern is not so much what happens today when people go in and buy voice scramblers," said Baker, a dapper, mustached lawyer who worked as an Education Department lawyer in the Carter Administration. "It is the prospect that in 5 years or 10 years every phone you buy that costs $75 or more will have an encrypt button on it that will interoperate with every other phone in the country and suddenly we will discover that our entire communications network is being used in ways that are profoundly antisocial. That's the real concern, I think, that Clipper addresses. If we are going to have a standardized form of encryption that is going to change the world, we should think seriously about what we are going to do when it is misused."

Not all law-enforcement experts believe that cryptography will unleash a riot of lawlessness. William R. Spernow, a Sacramento, Calif., computer crime specialist who works on a grant from the Federal Bureau of Justice Assistance, has encountered a few cases in which criminals have encrypted information unbreakably, including one involving a pedophile who encrypted the identities of his young victims. Yet Spernow sees no reason to panic. "In cases where there's encryption, the officers have been able to make the case through other investigative means," he says. "If we hustle, we can still make our cases through other kinds of police work."

But crime is only part of the problem. What happens to national security if cryptography runs free? Those who know best, officials of the National Security Agency, won't say. When the agency's director, Vice Adm. John M. McConnell testified before a Senate subcommittee on May 3, he withheld comment on this question until the public hearing was terminated and a second, classified session convened in a secure room.

Still, the effect of strong crypto on N.S.A. operations is not difficult to imagine. The agency is charged with signals intelligence, and it is widely assumed that it monitors all the communications between borders and probably much of the traffic within foreign countries. (It is barred from intercepting domestic communications.) If the crypto revolution crippled N.S.A.'s ability to listen in on the world, the agency might miss out on something vital—for instance, portents of a major terrorist attack.

No compelling case has been made, however, that the key-escrow system would make it easier for authorities to learn of such an attack. The National Security Agency would take the legal steps to seek the telltale keys after it had first identified those potential terrorists and wiretapped their calls, then discovered the inpenetrable hiss of encryption. Even then, the keys would be useful only if the terrorists were encoding conversations with Clipper technology, the one kind the Government had the capability to decode instantly. What sort of nuclear terrorist would choose Clipper?

The Government response has been to say that potential terrorists might indeed use alternative crypto methods to converse among themselves. But if Clipper were the accepted standard, the terrorists would have to use it to communicate with outsiders—banks, suppliers and other contacts. The Government could listen in on those calls. However, the work of the Bell Labs researcher, Matthew Blaze, casts serious doubt on that contention. Blaze has uncovered a flaw in Clipper that would allow a user to bypass the security funtion of the chip. Anyone who tinkered with Clipper in this way could communicate in privacy with anyone else with a Clipper phone and Government wiretappers would be unable to locate the key to unscramble the conversations.

Nonetheless, it was the terrorist threat, along with national security concerns, that moved the Clinton Administration to support the key-escrow initiative. White House high-tech policy makers share a recurrent fear: one day they might be sitting before an emergency Congressional investigation after the destruction of half of Manhattan by a stolen nuclear weapon planted in the World Trade towers and trying to explain that the Government had intercepted the communications of the terrorists but could not understand them because they used strong encryption. If Clipper were enacted, they could at least say, "We tried."

Obviously the Government views the Crypto revolution with alarm and wants to contain it. For years, much of its efforts have focused on the use of stringent export controls. While cryptography within the United States is unrestricted, the country's export laws treat any sort of encryption as munitions, like howitzers or nuclear triggers. The National Security Agency is the final arbiter and it will approve exports of cryptosystems in computer software and electronic hardware only if the protective codes are significantly weakened.

The N.S.A. stance is under attack from American businesses losing sales to foreign competitors. Listen to D. James Bidzos, the 39-year-old president of RSA Data Security, the Redwood City, Calif., company that controls the patents for public-key cryptography: "For almost 10 years, I've been going toe to toe with these people at Fort Meade. The success of this company is the worst thing that can happen to them. To them, we're the real enemy, we're the real target."

RSA is making a pitch to become the standard in encryption; its technology has been adopted by Apple, AT&T, Lotus, Microsoft, Novell and other major manufacturers. So imagine its unhappiness that its main rival is not another private company, but the National Security Agency, designer of the key-escrow cryptosystems. The agency is a powerful and dedicated competitor.

"We have the system that they're most afraid of," Bidzos says. "If the U.S. adopted RSA as a standard, you would have a truly international, interoperable, unbreakable, easy-to-use encryption technology. And all those things together are so synergistically theatening to the N.S.A.'s interests that it's driving them into a frenzy."

The export laws put shackles on Bidzos's company while his overseas competitors have no such restaints. Cryptographic algorithms that the N.S.A. bans for export are widely published and are literally being sold on the streets of Moscow. "We did a study on the problem and located 340 foreign cryptographic products sold by foreign countries," says Douglas R. Miller, government affairs manager of the Software Publishers Association. "The only effect of export controls is to cripple our ability to compete."

The real potential losses, though, come not in the stand-alone encryption category, but in broader applications. Companies like Microsoft, Apple and Lotus want to put strong encryption into their products but cannot get licenses to export them. Often, software companies wind up installing a weaker brand of crypto in all their products so that they can sell a single version worldwide. This seems to be the Government's intent—to encourage "crypto lite," strong enough to protect communications from casual intruders but not from Government itself.

In the long run, however, export regulation will not solve the National Security Agency's problem. The crypto business is exploding. People are becoming more aware of the vunerability of phone conversations, particularly wireless ones. Even the National Football League is adopting crypto technology; it will try out encrypted radio communication between coaches and quarterbacks, so rivals can't intercept last-minute audibles.

Anticipating such a boom, the N.S.A. devised a strategy for the 90's. It would concede the need for strong encryption but encourage a system with a key-escrow "back door" that provides access to communications for itself and law enforcement. The security agency had already developed a strong cryptosystem based on an algorithm called Skipjack, supposedly 16 million times stronger than the previous standard, D.E.S. (Data Encryption Standard). Now the agency's designers integrated Skipjack into a new system that uses a Law Enforcement Access Field (LEAF) that adds a signal to the message that directs a potential wiretapper to the appropriate key to decipher the message. These features were included in a chip called Capstone, which could handle not only telephone communications but computer data transfers and digital signatures.

Supposedly, this technology was designed for Government use, but in 1993 the National Security Agency had a sudden opportunity to thrust it into the marketplace. AT&T had come to the agency with a new, relatively low-cost secure-phone device called the Security 3600 that was designed to use the nonexportable DES encryption algorithm. The N.S.A. suggested that perhaps AT&T could try something else: a stripped-down version of Capstone for telephone communications. This was the Clipper chip. As a result, AT&T got two things: an agreement that Uncle Sam would buy thousands of phones for its own use (the initial commitment was 9,000, from the F.B.I.) and the prospect that the phone would not suffer the unhappy fate of some other secure devices when considered for export. There was also the expectation that AT&T would sell a lot more phones, since private companies would need to buy Clipper-equipped devices to communicate with the Government's Clipper phones.

It was an ingenious plan for several reasons. By agreeing to buy thousands of phones, and holding out the promise that thousands, or even millions more might be sold, AT&T phones gained a price advantage that comes with volume. (The original price of the Surity 3600 was $1,195, considerably less than the previous generation of secure phones; Mykotronx, the company making the Clipper chip, says that each chip now costs $30, but in large orders could quickly go as low as $10.) That would give the phones a big push in the marketplace. But by saturating the market, Clipper had a chance to become the standard for encryption, depending on whether businesses and individuals would be willing to accept a device that had the compromise of a government-controlled back door.

This compromise, of course, is the essence of Clipper. The Government recognizes the importance of keeping business secrets, intimate information and personal data hidden from most eyes and ears. But it also preserves a means of getting hold of that information after obtaining "legal authorization, normally a court order," according to a White House description.

The N.S.A. presented the idea to the Bush Administration,

which took no action before the election. Then it had to convince a Democratic Administration to adopt the scheme, and started briefing the Clinton people during the transition. Many in the computer industry figured that with Vice President Al Gore's enthusiastic endorsement of the high-frontier virtues of the information highway, the Administration would never adopt any proposal so tilted in favor of law enforcement and away from his allies in the information industries. They figured wrong. A little more than two months after taking office, the Clinton Administration announced the existence of the Clipper chip and directed the National Institute of Standards and Technology to consider it as a Government standard.

Clipper was something the Administration—starting with the Vice President—felt compelled to adopt, and key escrow was considered an honorable attempt to balance two painfully contradictory interests, privacy and safety.

The reaction was instant, bitter and ceaseless. The most pervasive criticisms challenged the idea that a Clipper would be, as the standard said, "voluntary." The Government's stated intent is to manipulate the marketplace so that it will adopt an otherwise unpalatable scheme and make it the standard. Existing systems have to cope with export regulations and, now, incompatibility with the new Government Clipper standard. Is it fair to call a system voluntary if the Government puts all sorts of obstacles in the way of its competitors?

Others felt that it was only a matter of time before the National Security Agency pressured the Government to require key escrow of all cryptographic devices—that Clipper was only the first step in a master plan to give Uncle Sam a key to everyone's cyberspace back door.

"That's a real fear," says Stephen T. Walker, a former N.S.A. employee who is now president of Trusted Information Systems, a company specializing in computer security products. "I don't think the Government could pull it off—it would be like prohibition, only worse. But I think they might try it."

But mostly, people were unhappy with the essence of Clipper, that the Government would escrow their keys. As Diffie notes, key escrow reintroduces the vulnerability that led him to invent public key cryptography—any system that relies on trusted third parties is, by definition, weaker than one that does not. Almost no one outside the Government likes the key-escrow idea. "We published the standard for 60 days of public comments," says F. Lynn McNulty, associate director for computer security at the National Institute of Standards and Technology. "We received 320 comments, only 2 of which were supportive."

Many people thought that in the face of such opposition, the Administration would quietly drop the Clipper proposal. They were dismayed by the Feb. 4 announcement of the adoption of Clipper as a Government standard. Administration officials knew they were alienating their natural allies in the construction of the information superhighway but felt they had no alternative. "This," said Michael R. Nelson, a White House technology official, "is the Bosnia of telecommunications."

If Clipper is the administration's Techno-Bosnia, the crypto equivalent of snipers are everywhere—in industry, among privacy lobbyists and even among Christian Fundamentalists. But the most passionate foes are the Cypherpunks. They have been meeting on the second Saturday of every month at the offices of Cygnus, a Silicon Valley company, assessing new ways they might sabotage Clipper. The group was co-founded in September 1992 by Eric Hughes, a 29-year-old freelance cryptogapher, and Tim May, a 42-year-old physicist who retired early and rich from the Intel company. Other Cypherpunk cells often meet simultaneously in six or seven locations around the world, but the main gathering place for Cypherpunks is the Internet, by means of an active mailing list in which members post as many as 100 electronic messages a day.

Cypherpunks share a few common premises. They assume that cryptography is a liberating tool, one that empowers individuals. They think that one of the most important uses of cryptography is to protect communications from the Government. Many of them believe that the Clipper is part of an overall initiative against cryptography that will culminate in Draconian control of the technology. And they consider it worth their time to fight, educating the general public and distributing cryptographic tools to obstruct such control.

Both Hughes and May have composed manifestos. Hughes's call to arms proclaims: "Cypherpunks write code. We know that someone has to write software to defend privacy, and since we can't get privacy unless we all do, we're going to write it."

May's document envisions a golden age in which strong cryptography belongs to all—an era of "crypto anarchism" that governments cannot contain. To May, cryptography is a tool that will not only bestow privacy on people but help rearrange the economic underpinnings of society.

"Combined with emerging information markets, cryptography will create a liquid market for any and all material that can be put into words and pictures," May's document says. "And just as a seemingly minor invention like barbed wire made possible the fencing-off of vast ranches and farms, thus altering forever the concepts of land and property rights in the frontier West, so too will the seemingly minor discovery out of an arcane branch of mathematics come to be the wire clippers which dismantle the barbed wire around intellectual property."

At a recent meeting, about 50 Cypherpunks packed into the Cygnus conference room, with dozens of others participating electronically from sites as distant as Cambridge, Mass., and San Diego. The meeting stretched for six hours, with discussions of hardware encryption schemes, methods to fight an electronic technique of identity forgery called "spoofing," the operation of "remailing" services, which allow people to post electronic messages anonymously—and various ways to fight Clipper.

While the Cypherpunks came up with possible anti-Clipper slogans for posters and buttons, a bearded crypto activist in wire-rim glasses named John Gilmore was outside the conference room, showing the latest sheaf of cryptography-related Freedom of Information documents he'd dragged out of Government files. Unearthing and circulating the hidden crypto treasures of the National Security Agency is a passion of Gilmore, an early employee of Sun Microsystems who left the company a multimillionaire. The Government once threatened to charge him with a felony for copying some unclassified-and-later-reclassified N.S.A. documents from a university library. After the story hit the newspapers, the Government once again declassified the documents.

"This country was founded as an open society, and we still have the remnants of that society," Gilmore says. "Will crypto tend to open it or close it? Our Government is building some of these tools for its own use, but they are unavailable—we have paid for cryptographic breakthroughs but they're classified. I wish I could hire 10 guys—cryptographers, librarians—to try to pry cryptography out of the dark ages."

Perhaps the most admired Cypherpunk is someone who says he is ineligible because he often wears a suit. He is Philip R. Zimmermann, a 40-year-old software engineer and cryptographic consultant from Boulder, Colo., who in 1991 cobbled together a cryptography program for computer data and electronic mail. "PGP," he called it, meaning Pretty Good Privacy, and he decided to give it away. Anticipating the Cypherpunk credo, Zimmermann hoped that the appearance of free cryptography would guarantee its continued use after a possible Government ban. One of the first people receiving the program placed it on a computer attached to the Internet and within days thousands of people had PGP. Now the program has been through several updates and is becoming sort of a people's standard for public key cryptography. So far, it appears that no one has been able to crack information encoded with PGP.

Like Diffie, Zimmermann developed a boyhood interest in crypto. "When I was a kid growing up in Miami, it was just kind of cool—secret messages and all," he says. Later, "computers made it possible to do ciphers in a practical manner." He was fascinated to hear of public key cryptography and during the mid-1980's he began experimenting with a system that would work on personal computers. With the help of some colleagues, he finally devised a strong system, albeit one that used some patented material from RSA Data Security. And then he heard about the Senate bill that proposed to limit a citizen's right to use strong encryption by requiring manufacturers to include back doors in their products. Zimmermann, formerly a nuclear freeze activist, felt that one of the most valuable potential uses of cryptography was to keep messages secret from the Government.

Zimmermann has put some political content into the documentation for his program: "If privacy is outlawed, only outlaws will have privacy. Intelligence agencies have access to good cryptographic technology. So do the big arms and drug traffickers. So do defense contractors, oil companies, and other corporate giants. But ordinary people and grassroots political organizations mostly have not had access to affordable "military grade" public-key cryptographic technology. Until now."

He has been told that Burmese freedom fighters learn PGP in jungle training camps on portable computers, using it to keep documents hidden from their oppressive Government. But his favorite letter comes from a person in Latvia, who informed him that his program was a favorite among one-time refuseniks in that former Soviet republic. "Let it never be," wrote his correspondent, "but if dictatorship takes over Russia, your PGP is widespread from Baltic to Far East now and will help democratic people if necessary."

Early last year, Zimmermann received a visit from two United States Customs Service agents. They wanted to know how it was that the strong encryption program PGP had found its way overseas with no export license. In the fall, he learned from his lawyer that he was a target of a grand jury investigation in San Jose, Calif. But even if the Feds should try to prosecute, they are likely to face a tough legal issue: Can it be a crime, in the process of legally distributing information in this country, to place it on an Internet computer site that is incidentally accessible to network users in other countries? There may well be a First Amendment issue here: Americans prize the right to circulate ideas, including those on software disks.

John Gilmore has discovered that Government lawyers have their own doubts about these issues. In some documents he sued to get, there are mid-1980's warnings by the Justice Department that the export controls on cryptography presented "sensitive constitutional issues." In one letter, an assistant attorney general warns that "the regulatory scheme extends too broadly into an area of protected First Amendment speech."

Perhaps taking Phil Zimmermann to court would not be the Government's best method for keeping the genie in the bottle.

The Clipper program has already begun. About once a month, four couriers with security clearances travel from Washington to the Torrance, Calif., headquarters of Mykotronx, which holds the contract to make Clipper chips. They travel in pairs, two from each escrow agency: the NIST and the Treasury Department. The redundancy is a requirement of a protocol known as Two-Person Integrity, used in situations like nuclear missile launches, where the stakes are too high to rely on one person.

The couriers wait while a Sun work station performs the calculations to generate the digital cryptographic keys that will be imprinted in the Clipper chips. Then it splits the keys into two pieces, separate number chains, and writes them on two floppy disks, each holding lists of "key splits." To reconstruct the keys imprinted on the chip, and thereby decode private conversations, you would need both sets of disks.

After being backed up, the sets of disks are separated, each one going with a pair of couriers. When the couriers return to their respective agencies, each set of disks is placed in a double-walled safe. The backup copies are placed in similar safes. There they wait, two stacks of floppy disks that grow each month, now holding about 20,000 key splits, the so-called back doors.

Will this number grow into the millions as the Government hopes? Ultimately the answer lies with the American public. Administration officials are confident that when the public contemplates scenarios like the Fortress in the Bronx or the Mushroom Cloud in Lower Manhattan, it will realize that allowing the Government to hold the keys is a relatively painless price to pay for safety and national security. They believe the public will eventually accept it in the same way it now views limited legal wiretapping. But so far the Administration hasn't recruited many prominent supporters. The main one is Dorothy Denning, a crypto expert who heads the computer science department at Georgetown University.

"...the public will eventually accept it in the same way it now views limited legal wiretapping."

Since endorsing Clipper (and advocating passage of the Digital Telephony initiative) Denning has been savagely attacked on the computer nets. Some of the language would wither a professional wrestler. "I've seen horrible things written about me," Denning says with a nervous smile. "I try to actually now avoid looking at them, because that's not what's important to me. What's important is that we end up doing the right thing with this. It was an accumulation of factors that led me to agree with Clipper, and the two most important areas, to me, are organized crime and terrorism. I was exposed to cases where wiretaps had actually stopped crimes in the making, and I started thinking, "If they didn't have this tool, some of these things might have happened." You know, I hate to use the word responsibility, but I actually feel some sense of responsibility to at least state my position to the extent so that people will understand it."

The opponents of Clipper are confident that the marketplace will vote against it. "The idea that the Government holds the keys to all our locks, before anyone has even been accused of committing a crime, doesn't parse with the public," says Jerry Berman, executive director of the Electronic Frontier Foundation. "It's not America." Senator Leahy hints that Congress might not stand for the Clinton Administration's attempt to construct the key-escrow system, at an estimated cost of $14 million dollars initially and $16 million annually. "If the Administration wants the money to set up and run the key-escrow facilities," he says, "it will need Congressional approval." Despite claims by the National Institute of Standards and Technology deputy director, Raymond G. Kammer, that some foreign governments have shown interest in the scheme, Leahy seems to agree with most American telecommunications and computer manufacturers that Clipper and subsequent escrow schemes will find no favor in the vast international marketplace, turning the United States into a cryptographic island and crippling important industries.

Leahy is also concerned about the Administration's haste. "The Administration is rushing to implement the Clipper chip program without thinking through crucial details," he says. Indeed, although the Government has been buying and using Clipper encryption devices, the process of actually getting the keys out of escrow and using them to decipher scrambled conversations has never been field tested. And there exists only a single uncompleted prototype of the device intended to do the deciphering.

Leahy is also among those who worry that, all policy issues aside, the Government's key escrow scheme might fail solely on technical issues. The Clipper and Capstone chips, while powerful enough to use on today's equipment, have not been engineered for the high speeds of the coming information highway; updates will be required. Even more serious are the potential design flaws in the unproved key-escrow scheme. Matthew Blaze's discovery that wrongdoers could foil wiretappers may be only the first indication that Clipper is unable to do the job for which it was designed. In his paper revealing the glitch, he writes, "It is not clear that it is possible to construct EES (Escrow Encryption Standard) that is both completely invulnerable to all kinds of exploitation as well as generally useful."

At bottom, many opponents of Clipper do not trust the Government. They are unimpressed by the elaborate key-escrow security arrangements outlined for Clipper. Instead, they ask questions about the process by which the Clipper was devised—how is it that the N.S.A., an intelligence agency whose mission does not ordinarily include consumer electronics design, has suddenly seized a central role in creating a national information matrix? They also complain that the Skipjack cryptographic algorithm is a classified secret, one that cryptographic professionals cannot subject to the rigorous, extended testing that has previously been used to gain universal trust for such a standard.

"You don't want to buy a set of car keys from a guy who specializes in stealing cars," says Marc Rotenberg, director of the Electronic Privacy Information Center. "The N.S.A.'s specialty is the ability to break codes, and they are saying, "Here, take our keys, we promise you they'll work."

At the March conference on computers and privacy, Stewart Baker responded to this sort of criticism. "This is the revenge of people who couldn't go to Woodstock because they had too much trig homework," he said, evoking some catcalls. "It's a kind of romanticism about privacy. The problem with it is that the beneficiaries of that sort of romanticism are going to be predators. PGP, they say, is out there to protect freedom fighters in Latvia. But the fact is, the only use that has come to the attention of law enforcement agencies is a guy who was using PGP so the police could not tell what little boys he had seduced over the net. Now that's what people will use this for—it's not the only thing people will use it for, but they will use it for that—and by insisting on having a claim to privacy that is beyond social regulation, we are creating a world in which people like that will flourish and be able to do more than they can do today."

Even if Clipper flops, the Crypto War will continue. The Administration remains committed to limiting the spread of strong cryptography unless there's a back door. Recently, it has taken to asking opponents for alternatives to Clipper. One suggestion it will not embrace is inaction. "Deciding that the genie is out of the bottle and throwing our arms up is not where we're at," says a White House official.

The National Security Agency will certainly not go away. "The agency is really worried about its screens going blank" due to unbreakable encryption, says Lance J. Hoffman, a professor of computer science at George Washington University. "When that happens, the N.S.A.—said to be the largest employer in Maryland—goes belly-up. A way to prevent this is to expand its mission and to become, effectively, the one-stop shop for encryption for Government and those that do business with the Government."

"The National Security Agency will certainly not go away."

Sure enough, the security agency is cooking up an entire product line of new key-escrow chips. At Fort Meade, it has already created a high-speed version of the Skipjack algorithm that outperforms both Clipper and Capstone. There is also another, more powerful, encryption device in the works named Baton. As far as the agency is concerned, these developments are no more than common sense. "To say that N.S.A. shouldn't be involved in this issue is to say that Government should try to solve this difficult technical and social problem with both hands tied behind its back," Stewart Baker says.

But Phil Zimmermann and the Cypherpunks aren't going away, either. Zimmermann is, among other things, soliciting funds for a PGP phone that will allow users the same sort of voice encryption provided by the Clipper chip. The difference, of course, is that in his phone there is no key escrow, no back door. If the F.B.I. initiated a wiretap on someone using Zimmermann's proposed phone, all the investigators would hear is static that they could never restore to orderly language.

What if that static shielded the murderous plans of a terrorist or kidnapper? Phil Zimmermann would feel terrible. Ultimately he has no answer. "I am worried about what might happen if unlimited security communications come about," he admits. "But I also think there are tremendous benefits. Some bad things would happen, but the trade-off would be worth it. You have to look at the big picture."

Policing Cyberspace[5]

When Ruth Warren's in-laws offered to buy a computer for her three children, she was both delighted and worried. Delighted, because she believed it would be an excellent educational tool. And worried because she knew it would not be long before her kids wanted to get on the Internet.

"We had heard there's a lot of awful stuff out there," says Warren, a homemaker and part-time piano teacher in Courtice, Ont., 50 km east of Toronto. "My neighbor told me how easy it is to find it—all you have to do is type in a search word and you're into really terrible pornography. I didn't want my kids to come across anything like that, even by mistake."

The explosion of Internet technology has created a catch-22 for parents: if they give the green light to Internet access, opening the door to a universe of fascinating and useful information, they also risk exposing their kids to hard-core pornography and other information many would deem inappropriate. A far cry from the boyhood staple of a dog-eared copy of Playboy wedged under a mattress, pornography on the Internet can include pictures and text about everything from bizarre fetishes to prostitution to pedophilia—material that would shock many adults, let alone their children. And the nastiness does not stop there: violence, hate literature, cult information and drug lore have also seeped onto the Net and its cyberspace sibling, the World Wide Web.

While some computer users dismiss the concern over smut on the Internet as overblown, on-line censorship is now a hotly debated topic, prompting several attempts at regulation. Last week, President Bill Clinton signed into law a sweeping telecommunications bill that imposes fines of up to $340,000 and as long as five years in prison on anyone who transmits "indecent material" over a public computer network to which minors have access. (In Canada, the Criminal Code makes it an offense to distribute, by any means, material whose dominant characteristic "is the undue exploitation of sex.") And at the end of December, CompuServe, a major commercial on-line service, blocked worldwide access to 200 electronic newsgroups after it was accused of breaking German law by allowing access to illegal material, including child pornography.

Those restrictions have prompted an angry backlash. The American Civil Liberties Union has filed suit against the U.S. government, charging that the crackdown on indecent material violates free speech. In addition, many individual Internet users resent government intervention, and believe the responsibility for the safety and well-being of children belongs in the hands of

5 Article by Sara Curtis, from *Maclean's* 109:56-7 F 19, '96. Copyright © 1996 *Maclean's*. Reprinted with permission.

parents, not politicians. Their view is that individual computer users should decide what is appropriate for their children.

Ruth Warren agrees. Her kids now surf the Net with CYBERsitter, one of several software products that are designed to help parents monitor and control their children's Internet use. Designed by Solid Oak Software of Santa Barbara, Calif., CYBERsitter is a Windows program featuring a "filter file" that lists Web pages, newsgroups and other Net sites devoted to sex, drugs, racism, violence or other illegal, adult-oriented or potentially offensive activities. Users can add to the file, but cannot delete any of the items that are already on the list. When loaded and activated, the program prevents access to any of the forbidden sites, and it can alert parents to attempted access of those sites. CYBERsitter will also disallow certain words or phrases for use on the Internet or in e-mail, including the child's name, address, or phone number.

"CYBERsitter has really given us peace of mind," says Warren, whose three children, between the ages of 12 and 15, are on the Internet daily. Warren and her husband, Carl, received CYBERsitter as part of a package with their subscription to Worldwide Online, a local Internet access provider. "We had been looking around at similar products in the stores, and had decided we wouldn't go on the Internet until we had one of these programs in place. Without it we would have been worried all the time."

"CYBERsitter is one of several parental control software programs on the market...."

CYBERsitter is one of several parental control software programs on the market, all of which seek to limit access to children by blocking specified sites or words. Another popular product, SurfWatch, available from SurfWatch Software in Los Altos, Calif., also blocks Web, chat and similar sites, but its "filter set" of more than 2,000 sites includes only those of a sexual nature, and does not allow parents to add or delete files as they wish. Since new Web sites appear daily, many parents may want to update the list of censored sites regularly. SurfWatch updates its group of sites monthly, and charges $8 a month to receive those updates (by contrast, CYBERsitter's updates can be downloaded from the company's Web site for free). An upgraded version of SurfWatch, due out in six weeks, will allow parents to add and delete words and sites, as well as to select sites from other categories, such as violence, alcohol and drugs, and gambling. Surf-Watch is available for both Macintosh and Windows.

Another option is Cyber Patrol, also for both Windows and Macintosh, from Microsystems Software Inc. of Framingham, Mass. Cyber Patrol comes loaded with a "CyberNOT Block List," which prohibits access to 6,000 different sites, divided into categories such as Sexual Acts/Text, Racist/Ethnic, and Violence/Profanity. Parents can add sites or unlock sites that are on the CyberNOT list. Cyber Patrol also allows parents to restrict access to certain times of day, limit total time spent on-line per day or week, and control access to online providers and local applications such as games and personal financial managers. For $3.50 a month, Cyber Patrol will automatically dial up the company and update the CyberNOT list every seven days. The current version of Cyber Patrol does not log on-line activity, but the next version will. It will also require a different password for each child, allowing adults to customize access to categories and services.

Two other popular products are Canadian. The Internet Filter, a Windows program from Vancouver-based Turner Investigations, Research and Communications, comes with a fully configurable dictionary of sites and vocabulary, and logs all inappropriate access attempts by the child. However, the company does not provide updates to the dictionary. What Internet Filter does offer is the option of alerting parents—by sending an e-mail message to another computer, say, at the office—when a child has attempted to access forbidden material. The next version will log all e-mail transactions and allow users to post warnings about new adult-oriented sites on the company's home page, where they can be retrieved by other users.

"Updates can be downloaded free of charge from the Net Nanny home page."

Finally, Net Nanny, by Trove Investment Corp. of Vancouver, is another Windows program that comes with a dictionary of forbidden Web sites, newsgroups and chat rooms, to which parents can add or delete. Updates can be downloaded free of charge from the Net Nanny home page. As well as logging activity, it can also prevent a name, address, phone number or credit card number from being given out over the Internet. And it has a two-way, real-time screening tool, which filters all conversations coming in and going out of the computer. For example, if someone in a chat room asks the child where he lives, the computer automatically shuts down.

However, Net Nanny does not stop at Internet activity. It will screen phone numbers dialled by the modem, and block access to games and other specified files on the hard drive, as well as the floppy and cd-rom drives. "Basically, it monitors everything the computer does," says Gordon Ross, president and chief executive officer of Trove. "We focus on the heart of the computer, not just the Internet." The aim, in short, is to put parents' minds at ease.

SAFE SURFING:
CYBERsitter
Parents can add to preset menu of forbidden sites and words, but not delete.
Solid Oak Software Inc. (800) 388-2761
Windows only
$54, free updates

SurfWatch
List of censored sites only includes material of a sexual nature, and parents cannot add or delete.
SurfWatch Software Inc. (800) 458-6600

Windows and Macintosh
$69, plus $8/month for updates

Cyber Patrol
Can restrict access to certain times of day and limit total time spent on-line.
Microsystems Software Inc. (800) 828-2608
Windows and Macintosh
$69, plus $3.50/month for automatic updates

The Internet Filter
Can be set to alert parent by e-mail if child attempts access to forbidden material.
Turner Investigations, Research and Communications. (604) 733-5095
Windows only
$49.95, no updates

Net Nanny
Includes two-way, real-time screening tool that filters material sent or received by the computer.
Trove Investment Corp. (800) 340-7177
Windows only
$49.95, free updates

Bibliography

An asterisk (*) preceding a reference indicates that an excerpt from the work has been reprinted in this compilation.

Books and Pamphlets

Adler, Allan R., ed. Litigation under the federal freedom of information act and privacy act. ACLU. '90.

Alderman, Ellen, and Kennedy, Caroline. The right to privacy. Knopf. '95.

Bacard, Andre. The computer privacy handbook. Peachpit Press. '96.

Banigar, David, and Rotenberg, Marc, eds. Cryptography and privacy sourcebook: primary documents on U. S. encryption policy, the clipper chip, the digital telephony proposal and export controls. Diane. '94.

Bielefield, Arlene, and Cheeseman, Lawrence. Maintaining the privacy of library records: a handbook and guide. Neal and Schuman. '94.

Bollas, Christopher, and Sundelson, David. The new informants: the betrayal of confidentiality in psychoanalysis and psychotherapy. J. Aronson. '95.

Branscomb, Anne Wells. Who owns information? From privacy to public access. Basic. '95.

Bruce, JoAnne C. Privacy and confidentiality of health-care information. American Hospital Publications. '96.

Decker, Kurt H. Privacy in the workplace: rights, procedures and policies. LRP Publishers. '94.

Dickinson, Philip D. Employee privacy rights and wrongs. M. Lee Smith. '96.

Dolan, Edward F. Your privacy: protecting it in a nosy world. Dutton. '95.

Donaldson, Molla S, and Lohr, Kathleeen N., eds. Health data in the information age: use, disclosure, and privacy. National Academy Press. '94.

Garrow, David J. Liberty and sexuality: the right to privacy and the making of Roe v. Wade, Simon & Schuster, '94.

Gottfried, Ted. Privacy: individual right vs. social needs. Millbrook Press. '94.

Inness, Julie. Privacy, intimacy, and isolation. Oxford University Press. '96.

La Fave, Wayne R. Search and seizure: a treatise on the fourth amendment. West. '96.

Liddell, Grantt. The privacy act. Oxford University Press. '95.

Lyon, David. The electronic eye: the rise of surveillance society. University of Minnesota Press. '94.

Mc Lean, Deckle. Privacy and its invasion. Praeger. '95.

Neumann, Peter G. Computer-related risks. Addison-Wesley. '95.

Schneier, Bruce. E-Mail security: how to keep your electronic messages private. Wiley. '95.

Schwartau, Winn. Information warfare: chaos on the electronic superhighway. Thunder's Mouth. '96.

Scott, Gini Graham. Mind your own business: the battle for personal privacy. DaCapo. '95.

Shannon, M. L. The paper trail: personal and financial privacy in the nineties. Lysias Press. '95.

Smith, H. Jeff. Managing privacy: information technology, and corporate America. University of North Carolina Press. '94.

Stallings, William. Network and internetwork security: principles and practice.

Macmillan. '95.
——. Protect your privacy: the PGP user's guide. Prentice-Hall. '94.
Zigarelli, Michael A. Can they do that? A guide to your rights on the job. Free Press.
  '94.

Additional Periodical Articles with Abstracts

Shrink and tell. Is your confidentiality being compromised? Lisa Collier Cool. *American Health for Women* 15:16-18 D '96

Managed-care plans covering psychotherapy are demanding increasingly intimate information about subscribers' emotional problems before approving treatment. According to Harold Eist, president of the American Psychiatric Association, these policies are trampling on the privacy of psychiatric patients and jeopardizing their quality of care. As a result, the American Psychoanalytic Association has urged its members not to reveal anything divulged during treatment sessions, and other pyschiatric organizations have boycotted managed health care companies entirely. David Olsen of Health Systems International, California, counters that this information is required to monitor the quality of care and to make sure it is appropriate. Managed-care advocates also add that unless someone holds therapists accountable, patients might spend years at sessions with no improvement. Some new regulations dealing with breaches in privacy are discussed.

Another excuse to trash newsrooms. Jane E. Kirtley. *American Journalism Review* 18:54 S '96

The amendment to the federal Privacy Protection Act of 1980 proposed in Senator Orrin Hatch's bill, which was directed toward allowing searches for child pornography, poses a direct threat to press freedom. The Privacy Protection Act specifically forbids searches of people in the media when the alleged crime involves ownership or dissemination of written materials, unless the documents contain classified national security information. Hatch wants to introduce an exemption that would include anything that meets the new definition of child pornography, which includes imaginary and morphed depictions of children engaged in sexually explicit acts. This amendment would merely give law enforcement officials, who are already zealous enough in chasing evidence, another excuse to trash America's newsrooms.

Privacy issues frame pilot records debate. Edward H. Phillips. *Aviation Week & Space Technology* 144:34 Ja 1 '96

Airline industry officials are asking Congress to be cautious about legislation dealing with the accessibility of pilot employment records. The U.S. National Transportation Safety Board wants standardized information about pilot qualifications to be maintained and shared among airlines and independent training agencies. Safety board officials made the recommendations after investigating the crash of an American Eagle regional transport in December 1994. They found previous deficiencies in the pilot's flying performance that were unknown to American Eagle. Airline industry officials support access to employment records by prospective employers, but they are concerned about "thorny privacy, defamation, negligence, and contract interference issues" that must be dealt with to protect both the airlines and pilots, according to Edward Merlis, senior vice president of the Air Transport Association.

High resolution, unresolved. Mary Graham. *Atlantic Monthly* 278:24+ Jl '96

The commercial use of spy satellites raises a number of concerns about national security, the protection of privacy, and public access to information. In 1994, the Clinton administration decided to allow private companies to launch satellites with high-resolution sensors that had previously been available only to the intelligence community. The administration also ruled that these companies could provide information to anyone who would pay for it. Four American firms are now hurrying to launch satellites of their own equipped with such technology. The making of precise maps that connect the physical characteristics of residences with other publicly available information should be limited by the traditional idea that a person's home and surrounding areas are private. In addition, commercial satellite projects should be restricted by the concept that geographic data is a national resource, to be shared at minimal cost.

Big breakthrough or Big Brother? John Carey. *Business Week* 88+ N 18 '96

Industry and government may be close to a solution to a fierce policy debate that sets the needs of law enforcement against the right to privacy. In October, the Clintonites decreed that firms could now export even the strongest computer cryptography programs, as long as companies maintain access to their own decoding keys and provide them in response to warrants or court orders. The new policy gave rise to opposition among everyone from privacy advocates and right-wing conservatives to some software executives. Many experts predict that industry will ultimately go along, however, contending that much current criticism represents a simple lack of understanding of the companies' own need to "recover," or access, encoding keys. Although communications software needs to be adapted, the administration is currently drafting a bill that would clarify liability issues for key-recovery centers. Whether the idea becomes a global solution also depends on other governments' acceptance of it. The latest generation of computer cryptography is explained.

How to practice safe surfing. Edward C. Baig. *Business Week* 120-1 S 9 '96

There is a lot of information available on the millions of people who surf the Net, and a person need not be a hacker to access it. This information, if it is in the hands of someone like an ex-lover or a voyeur, can be used against a person, and more commonly, it can be used by companies to sketch a demographic profile of a person based on their on-line habits. Messages posted in the public Usenet forum live on in the search-engine archives for anyone to exploit, and even communications that people think are private and anonymous can make their way to many potential snoopers. The writer discusses how consumers can take a variety of common sense steps to safeguard their privacy, observing that if people practice common sense and report trouble immediately, they should be able to maintain a reasonable shield of privacy while still getting all the benefits of the Internet.

Privacy and the 'cookie' monster. Stephen H. Wildstrom. *Business Week* 22 D 16 '96

By using bits of data on a computer's hard drive, World Wide Web sites can keep track of a visitor's activities. Known as cookies, these pieces of information are potent devices for Web-site designers, because a Web server can customize content if it can determine whether visitors have been to a site before and what they have seen. Controversy arises when cookies are used for more than bookkeeping, however. Some site owners sell information gleaned from cookies to advertisers and other interested parties. Many people object to this prying and marketing, particularly when it is carried out without their knowledge or consent. The writer explains how to delete cookies from a hard drive.

They're watching you online. Stephen H.Wildstrom. *Business Week* 19 N 11 '96

Growing concern about privacy on the Internet is increasing the chance that restrictions will be imposed by the government. Privacy worries range from the gathering and distribution of personal information on the World Wide Web—which can be gold to marketers, for example, particularly as the Web enables a user's on-line behavior to be monitored—to employers' ability to eavesdrop on every detail of employees' computer use. Although the legal status of the latter is unclear, Federal Trade Commissioner Christine A. Varney warned recently that unless on-line businesses restrict their own collection of data, especially from children, the government will.

It can't happen here. Brigid McMenamin. *Forbes* 157:252 + My 20 '96

A new central database will eventually contain a complete medical and psychological profile of every resident of Maryland. For the past year, 12 of the largest medical claim payers in the state have been quietly sending private medical and, in some incidences, psychiatric claims to the Maryland Department of Mental Health & Hygiene. The information is being stored in a new computer system called the Medical Care Data Base. Before long every Maryland doctor, chiropractor, psychologist, and psychiatrist will be obliged to report every patient visit to the data bank. Although officials of the Maryland Health Care Access & Cost Commission claim that the database represents an effort to curb health care costs, the reality is that they are trying to control doctors. The Maryland reformers are planning to use the database to oversee procedures and control the use of what they perceive as unnecessary treatments. A sidebar offers advice on protecting your private medical records.

Techno-hero or public enemy? David Stipp. *Fortune* 134:172-4 + N 11 '96

The right to privacy and the health of the U.S. software industry is at stake in the conflict between RSA Data Security and the U.S. National Security Agency (NSA). RSA makes software that is integrated into about 90 million copies of various applications and becoming ubiquitous. Its power arises from encryption, which scrambles data transmitted over phone lines or stored in computers so that access is limited to those in possession of secret numerical "keys." The government is uneasy about this capacity. Law enforcers are worried that the technology will be used to prevent them from eavesdropping on wrongdoers. Moreover, the NSA is concerned that a "strong" version of this software could be used to tie their operations in knots, and they want to stop CEO James Bidzos from going global with his company's product.

The fight to legislate incompetence out of the cockpit. Ronald B. Lieber. *Fortune* 133:30 F 5 '96

The National Transportation Safety Board has begged Congress to resolve the current situation whereby airline companies that pass along information about a pilot's safety and performance record to another airline can be sued for invasion of privacy. This situation has cost dozens of lives through disasters caused by pilot ineptitude, and the Senate and the House now have new bills before them that would protect airlines from liability for sharing performance records. A bill may be passed this spring, but at the moment there is conflict over whether the airlines or the government should maintain the records. The Air Line Pilots Association wants the records kept away from the FAA, and FAA administrator David Hinson, who is in the process of streamlining the agency, believes that the records should be a company matter.

The "nuts and sluts" strategy. Tamar Stieber. *Glamour* 94:138 Ag '96

The writer recounts how, after filing a sex-discrimination suit against her employer, her sex life and medical records came under scrutiny and she became the subject of a ferocious campaign of intimidation. She maintains that the Civil Rights Act of 1991, which aims to help victims by allowing juries to award damages to women who suffer emotional distress as a result of sex discrimination, actually opened the door for the intrusion she suffered. As the financial stakes have risen, she explains, so has employers' investment in winning the cases; one way of doing so, she points out, is to prove that a woman already had emotional problems and that her treatment at work was not to blame.

Private people, public lives. Martha Sherrill. *Harper's Bazaar* 126+ N '95

In their new book, *The Right to Privacy*, Ellen Alderman and Caroline Kennedy discuss the erosion of privacy in people's lives. They focus on ordinary, unfamous individuals and address the gray areas where the law has yet to protect with certainty. The cases they discuss give rise to concern about physical privacy, cyberprivacy, and even the privacy of fertilized pre-embryos. According to Alderman, the more research she and Kennedy conducted, the more apparent it became that privacy enables people to make fundamental decisions about their lives and to decide who they want to be.

The coming battle for customer information. John Hagel, III and Jeffrey F. Rayport. *Harvard Business Review* 75:53-5+ Ja/F '97

As consumers take control of the information that businesses have about them, access to it could become costly and complex. Consumers who are edgy about the amount and depth of information businesses collect about them are going to take ownership of the data and demand value in exchange for it. Companies aware of the potential for change, meanwhile, will ensure that they continue to obtain the information they need in order to compete in the 21st century. The writers discuss new technologies that will allow consumers to capture extensive profiles of their own activities and decide whether to release the data.

Should AIDS tests be mandatory for pregnant women? S. Kuvin and J. Stryker. *Health* 10:28 Ja/F '96

AIDS tests for pregnant women are voluntary under current federal guidelines, but some lawmakers and doctors say that this does not go far enough to ensure the health of newborns. An infectious disease physician and a medical ethicist offer arguments for and against the proposition that AIDS tests should be mandatory for pregnant women.

Cloaks and daggers. Peter H. Lewis. *Home Office Computing* 14:133 Jl '96

Many people believe that some of the most troubling social problems on the Internet and on-line information services could be eliminated, or at least curtailed, if people were obliged to use their real names in cyberspace. Despite a rising number of abuses in the electronic world, anonymity and pseudonymity are valued traditions in America, and the Supreme Court has supported the right to speak anonymously, as long as the speech itself does not breach any law. The use of anonymity deserves protection, even when it is used as a mask to hide behind when doing foul and illegal things. That said, there is nothing preventing the on-line services from trying to clean up their own electronic systems by banning the use of screen names—except of course a loss of revenue if large numbers of subscribers decided to log on where they can speak anonymously.

UMass settles invasion of privacy complaint from basketball players. *Jet* 90:19 Ag 12 '96

Six former and current members of the University of Massachusetts basketball team will receive a financial award from the school after their grades were leaked to the news media and eventually published. The players claimed that their privacy was violated when their grades were published by the Boston Globe in 1994. A statement claimed that the leaking of the players' grades led to the widespread publication of a series of reports, which the players believed seriously misrepresented their academic commitments and abilities. The Boston Globe reported that the claim was settled for $72,000.

A duty to defy foolish regulations. Barbara Amiel. *Maclean's* 109:9 Ag 12 '96

Over the last seven weeks, D. Bruce Petrie, assistant chief statistician at Census Canada, and columnist George Jonas have, in the Toronto *Sun*, debated the 1996 census questionnaire. Jonas contends that the census is overly intrusive, that the confidentiality of the information cannot be maintained, and that decent citizens ought not to fill it out. Petrie, however, disagrees with these views, noting that all the information is required and that Statistics Canada takes seriously its legal obligation to safeguard the privacy and confidentiality of all respondents. Ways in which the census could be improved are discussed.

Progress report on the information superhighway. Clarence Irving. *Macworld* 13:260 Mr '96

Last October, the National Telecommunications and Information Administration released a white paper in response to consumers' growing concerns about Internet privacy. This white paper suggests a framework for creating minimum privacy standards that communications and information service providers, such as phone companies and video and on-line services, would implement to protect any personal information their subscribers generate. Informed consent is vital to this framework, and the plan's success relies on service providers' willingness to be self-regulating. Before selling information that a consumer has disclosed to gain access to the network, or using that data for any non-service-related purpose, a service provider should have to reveal how it intends to use the information and obtain the customer's consent.

HIV testing: keeping it confidential. Whitney Walker. *Ms.* 6:32 Ja/F '96

Knowing how the various methods work eases the traumatic process of testing for HIV. Tests can be made anonymously, confidentially, or through one's own doctor (a home HIV test kit is awaiting FDA sanction). Each method offers varying degrees of confidentiality and protection when it comes to insurance companies or employers having access to the medical records of the person being tested. In some cases, insurance companies have dropped a person's policy simply for being tested, even if the result was negative, as they assumed that person was at risk. Similarly, the results of tests held by a company doctor or an in-house benefits administrator may be shared with the employer. In some states, insurance companies can decide not to honor medical claims for "preexisting conditions" such as HIV. Information and recommendations with regard to testing and confidentiality are provided.

No kidding. Alexandra Socarides. *Ms.* 7:25 S/O '96

Kids Off Lists (KOL) is an organization that aims to show parents how to recall information that firms may have on their families and how to avoid future data-bashing of their children. The idea for the organization was that of Marc Klaas, father of murdered 12-year-old Polly Klaas. Metromail, a direct-mail and consumer information company in Lombard, Illinois, that has data on 90 percent of American households and adds 67,000 babies' names every week, is the main target of KOL. The group also works with Senator Dianne Feinstein and Representative Bob Franks to pass the Children's Protection and Parental Empowerment Act of 1996.

Bad publicity. Jean Bethke Elshtain. *The New Republic* 215:25 Ag 12 '96

The politics of displacement is a political attitude that presumes an identity, rather than a relationship, between the personal and the political. If all conceptual boundaries are blurred and all distinctions between the private and the public abolished, however, no politics can exist by definition. A political perspective requires a differentiation between the activity called "politics"—that which is held in common and open to public scrutiny and judgment—from other activities and relationships. The total collapse of this distinction between private and public identities, commitments, and activities is anathema to democratic thinking, which regards these differences to be of critical importance.

Weighing the right to die. Larry Reibstein and Daniel Klaidman. *Newsweek* 129:62 Ja 13 '97

The Supreme Court will soon decide if doctors can help their patients kill themselves. The issue is a constitutional clash between personal autonomy and the state's interest in preserving life. Supporters argue that assisted suicide is a "fundamental right" protected by the 14th Amendment's due process clause, while opponents question whether this prospective right is in the "traditions" of the country. The basis of the states' argument is their responsibility to protect vulnerable groups who might be coerced into assisted suicide. The most likely result is for the Supreme Court to deny any right to suicide and in doing so clearly limit the right to privacy.

Another faulty encryption policy. *New York Times* A14 D 16 '96

The Clinton Administration's latest plan to control the export of encryption software is unworkable and risks trampling on privacy rights and harming American software companies. The Administration want to reserve the right to tap phone and computer messages without the caller's knowledge. This provision will compel foreign companies and individuals to buy encryption software from foreign companies.

A reasonable response to terror. *New York Times* A16 Jl 30 '96

In the wake of terrorist attacks, the leadership in Washington should resist the temptation to lunge for superficially attractive proposals that would undermine the liberties and privacy of Americans. President Clinton has urged Congress to take another look at several proposals that were ultimately not included in recent antiterrorism legislation.

Blessed ease, sweet privacy. Anita Gates. *New York Times* 14+ O 27 '96

Petit St. Vincent is a privately owned 113-acre island in the Grenadines suited to those who treasure their privacy. The 22-cottage resort is the only thing on the island, and room service is available for all three meals. The writer describes her stay at the expensive resort and the two planes and one boat ride required to reach it.

Cellular industry rejects U.S. plan for surveillance. John Markoff. *New York Times* A1 + S 20 '96

The wireless communications industry voted yesterday to reject Government-backed technology that would make it possible for law enforcement agencies to keep closer tabs on users of cellular telephones. The vote marks a showdown with the Justice Department, which contends that the Government has the right to use powerful new surveillance technology under a 1994 law to bring law enforcement techniques into the modern era.

Code set up to shield privacy of cellular calls is breached. John Markoff. *New York Times* A1 + Mr 20 '97

David Wagner, a University of California at Berkeley researcher, and Bruce Schneier and John Kelsey of Counterpane Systems, a consulting firm, announced today that they have cracked a key part of the electronic code meant to protect the privacy of calls made with the new, digital generation of cellular telephones. The announcement, which means that the new phones may in practice be little more secure from eavesdropping than the analog cellular phones in use the last 15 years, is intended as a public warning.

Company stops on-line access to key social security. Laurie Flynn. *New York Times* B11 Je 13 '96

After an onslaught of complaints, Lexis-Nexis has discontinued a new on-line offering that provided access to millions of individuals' Social Security numbers. According to company officials, Lexis-Nexis had expected law firms and law enforcement agencies to use the service for assistance in locating witnesses, heirs, or suspected criminals.

Corporate secrets. David F. Linowes *New York Times* A23 My 14 '96

A University of Illinois survey of 84 Fortune 500 companies found that 75 percent collected personal information about their employees. More than a third of the companies did not tell employees how such information was used, but a majority released the files to credit companies.

Easier passage. *New York Times* A32 Je 28 '96

Although the E-Z Pass system of electronic bridge toll payment has had a rocky debut, drivers will benefit when more people get passes. Meanwhile, bridge and tunnel officials need to use intelligent pricing variations for use of tokens to encourage more usage at non-peak hours, and the authorities must assure motorists that electronic billing and record-keeping will not invade their privacy.

'Filegate' may be good for us. Frank Askin. *New York Times* A13 Jl 8 '96

The Filegate scandal may ultimately do some good. Civil libertarians have long been concerned about the Government's extensive files on American citizens, but have been thwarted, mostly by Republican judges and politicians, in their attempts to rein in the practice. Now that the Republicans are expressing outrage over the Clinton Administration's abuse of F.B.I. files, there is hope that the average American can finally get some protection.

First Internet wiretap leads to a suspect. *New York Times* 20 Mr 31 '96

March 30) The first court-ordered wiretap on a computer network has provided evidence for Federal officials to charge Julio Cesar Ardita, an Argentine student, with hacking into U.S. military computers. Officials said he had gotten access to information about satellites, radiation, and engineering but he was not accused of stealing vital national secrets. They say the case shows their ability to track a computer criminal with court permission while maintaining the privacy of other computer users.

Hospital files as open book. Denise Grady. *New York Times* C8 Mr 12 '97

The University of Wisconsin hospital in Madison and the Beth Israel-Deaconess Medical Center in Boston have instituted systems to track employees who use the computer to spy on each other's medical records. So far, few other hospitals have instituted such computer security systems.

Justices uphold patient privacy with therapist. Linda Greenhouse. *New York Times* A1 + June 14 '96

(June 13) The Supreme Court ruled today that the Federal courts must permit psychotherapists and other mental health professionals to refuse to disclose patient records in judicial proceedings. The 7-to-2 ruling on Jaffee v. Redmond creates a new evidentiary privilege in both civil and criminal cases that is comparable to the lawyer-client and marital privileges that Federal courts have recognized for years. The Court's decision brings the Federal courts into line with the states, all of which currently recognize some form of psychotherapist-patient privilege.

Lawmakers agree on testing babies for the AIDS virus. Ian Fisher. *New York Times* A1 + May 1 '96

April 30—Sources say that House and Senate negotiators tentatively agreed today on legislation that would require states to require H.I.V. testing of newborns if health officials cannot reduce the number of infected infants by other means. Under the bill, states would lose federal money provided by the Ryan White act if they did not comply.

Lawsuit seeks to bar U.S. from access to AIDS files. Tamar Lewin. *New York Times* A13 Ap 3 '96

Boston social service agencies are scheduled to file a complaint in Federal District Court in Boston today to prevent Federal officials from obtaining records with the names and Social Security numbers of people with AIDS. The agencies claim that Federal auditors are involved in a grave breach of confidentiality when they collect such information about people enrolled in Federally funded programs.

Morris vs. Clinton. William Safire. *New York Times* A23 S 12 '96

It is ironic that Dick Morris, who let a prostitute eavesdrop on his conversation with President Clinton, is complaining about invasion of his privacy. However, Morris was an individual betraying his trust, while the Clinton administration, if retaliating, as Morris alleges, by wrongfully leaking confidential files would be a government abusing its powers.

National Enquirer faces trial on invasion-of-privacy issue. Linda Greenhouse. *New York Times* A22 D 5 '95

(Dec. 4) The Supreme Court refused today to consider whether California courts can allow damage suits for invasion of privacy over news articles that, while accurate, in a jury's view lack sufficient "social value" to be "newsworthy." The Justices turned down an appeal by *The National Enquirer*, the defendant in an invasion of privacy law-suit brought by the mother of an illegitimate son of the actor Eddie Murphy. The pub-lication had disclosed the existence of the mother and the 2-year-old child, as well as the financial arrangements that Murphy had made for his son.

Peeking at your P.C. Simson Garfinkel. *New York Times* 23 Ap 6 '96

"The Encrypted Communications Privacy Act of 1996" would increase the availability of good encryption software in the U.S., but it would limit people's freedoms in other ways. While lifting export controls, the act would criminalize certain uses of cryptog-raphy for the first time, and it also creates legal rules for "key holders"—organizations that would be given copies of an individual's decryption code.

Pioneers of cyberspace move into wider arena. Peter H. Lewis. *New York Times* A14 Ap 1 '96

(March 30) At the annual Computers, Freedom and Privacy Conference in Cambridge, Mass., some pioneers of the electronic frontier noted that as the masses have rushed to stake out claims on the Internet, the notion of a separate Net culture of computer wizards has vanished. But in their efforts to preserve the libertarian spirit of the Internet, these original members of the cyberspace community have emerged as a polit-ical and social force. In a clear sign of Internet users' new power, several members of Congress announced new legislation at the conference.

Private eyes and government files. *New York Times* 18 Jl 6 '96

Under a misguided reform proposed by Vice President Al Gore's "reinventing govern-ment" program, the Federal Government is getting ready to transfer 40 percent of its employee security checking to a private company. Some members have rightly ques-tioned whether the company will enjoy the confidence of state and local authorities and have wondered how the private entity will be monitored for compliance with Federal privacy laws.

Privacy legislation in Congress could wind up hindering research on drug use. Christopher Sale Wren. *New York Times* 12 My 19 '96

The Family Privacy Protection Act, passed by the House of Representatives last year and waiting on a final Senate vote, could hamper research into illegal drug use by American adolescents. The legislation, which was intended to protect children from questions about sex and other personal matters, requires written parental consent before minors are interviewed about their personal habits. Social scientists and some anti-drug activists say that the bill will prevent them from obtaining data on important issues.

Questions of privacy roil arena of psychotherapy. Tamar Lewin *New York Times* A1 + My 22 '96

Confidentiality is seen as a fundamental of psychotherapeutic treatment, giving patients the freedom to explore their innermost feelings and fantasies. However, the confidentiality of psychotherapy is being eroded by a wide variety of outside forces, including the spread of managed care, the computerization of medical records, and the use of therapists' notes and records in law enforcement.

Sex offenders law prompts privacy debate in New York. Monte Williams. *New York Times* 1 + F 24 '96

Under a law that went into effect on Jan. 21, citizens in New York can track the whereabouts of convicted sex offenders by calling a 900 telephone number or consulting a directory at police stations. The law has prompted a debate over privacy and public safety.

Simpson, in live cable interview, appeals to be allowed privacy. Bill Carter. *New York Times* A19 Ja 25 '96

In a live interview carried on the Black Entertainment Television cable channel, O.J. Simpson again declared his innocence and appealed to the public to allow him to pursue a living and the opportunity to play golf whenever he wants. The interview, broadcast on Wednesday night, was seen by about three million viewers.

Social security closes on-line site, citing risks to privacy. Robert Pear. *New York Times* A15 Ap 10 '97

The Social Security Administration shut down an Internet site that supplied information about individuals' personal income and retirement benefits because experts on computers and privacy law had expressed concern that it might violate privacy rights. The experts felt that the safeguards in place might not be enough to keep people from obtaining confidential electronic data about others. Acting Commissioner of Social Security John J. Callahan said yesterday that the agency will investigate other security features and then consider whether it should offer an on-line information service with such features.

Stand up for liberty. Anthony Lewis. *New York Times* A15 Ap 15 '96

Bill Clinton has compiled a poor record on civil liberties. A case in point is the counterterrorism bill, which includes a provision gutting Federal habeas corpus, the historic power of Federal courts to look into the constitutionality of state criminal proceedings. The President allowed this measure to be attached to the bill, and he has also supported legislation that would intrude on people's privacy.

Stay out of touch. William Safire. *New York Times* A23 Je 27 '96

The rage for pagers and cellular phones snatches away personal liberty. Reachability, which has become a value, will soon become an expectation, with those totally in touch becoming upset about privacy freaks who dare to self-isolate.

The DNA hard sell. Meredith Wadman. *New York Times* A15 D 16 '96

Congress should pass legislation that would protect medical privacy and prevent insurers and employers from discriminating on the basis of genetic information. Under current laws, there is nothing to prevent insurers from raising premiums on people who test positive for genetic mutations that predispose them to breast cancer and other diseases.

The governor's attack on the judges. *New York Times* 22 F 3 '96

Gov. George Pataki, moving to make crime a central issue for the State Legislature in an election year, has stepped up his attack on New York's seven-member Court of Appeals. This week he introduced legislation that would essentially strip the court of its authority to decide independently whether evidence obtained by the police should be suppressed as an unlawful seizure under the State Constitution. The measure would require that the court bow to rules set by the U.S. Supreme Court. It is of dubious constitutionality and deserves to be rejected as a threat to the individual liberty and privacy of every New Yorker.

'Their just powers.' William Safire. *New York Times* A19 Jl 4 '96

The growing protest at the invasion of privacy of nearly 1,000 Americans by the cesspool of snoopery, sudden death, and obstruction known as the Clinton Office of White House Counsel is being characterized as a mere "flap." This pattern of offenses, in a country that today celebrates its rebellion at the abuse of power, cannot be explained as stupendous stupidity.

Used computer bares old user's secrets. John Markoff. *New York Times* A14 Ap 4 '97

(April 3) When C.J. Prime bought a used IBM computer at an auction, she discovered it contained 2,000 patient records from Smitty's Supermarkets pharmacy in Tempe, Ariz. All the software the pharmacy had used for record keeping was still on the computer's hard disk, including patient names, addresses, Social Security numbers, and the medicine they had bought.

When confidentiality becomes a curse. *New York Times* A16 Ja 29 '96

A panel of the State Commission of Investigation has recommended changing confidentiality laws regarding investigation of child abuse and neglect. Such laws were intended to protect families' privacy, but too often shield social workers or impede the flow of information among concerned professionals. The state should move forward with these changes.

When patients' records are commodities for sale. Gina Kolata. *New York Times* A1 + N 15 '95

Individual medical records are increasingly being gathered and stored in commercial databanks maintained by such institutions as hospital networks, health maintenance organizations, and drug companies. There is a Federal law that protects the privacy of video rental lists, but private medical information is being bought and sold freely by companies that have ignored state laws that should have made it difficult to transfer those records across state lines.

Big Brother is us. James Gleick. *The New York Times Magazine* 130-2 S 29 '96

Part of a special issue on the next 100 years. As information gathering about individuals reaches an astonishing level of completeness, so have fears about the invasion of privacy. The breakneck expansion of the Internet surpasses the gloomiest predictions of interconnectedness. It also contradicts those forecasts. Oddly enough, the linking of computers has occurred democratically, even anarchically. Its rules and habits are unfolding in the open, rather than behind the closed doors of security agencies and corporate operations centers. It is obvious that technology has the potential not only to invade privacy but to safeguard it, through encryption for example, which will be available to all, as soon as the government steps out of the way. Moreover, despite opinion polls stating that Americans always favor privacy, most volunteer telephone numbers, mothers' maiden names, and even Social Security numbers to merchants promising discounts or Web services offering membership privileges. The issue of on-line anonymity is also discussed.

Keeping secrets. Maggie Scarf. *The New York Times Magazine* 38-41 Je 16 '96

As managed-care organizations demand increasingly detailed justifications for medical treatment and file more and more data electronically, the cloak of confidentiality that once protected psychotherapy has become increasingly threadbare. What happens between the patient and the therapist is singularly privileged, but at present it is unrealistic for people to assume that the sensitive issues they discuss will go no further, and many patients have become legitimately concerned about the possibility that what is being discussed could return to haunt them in cyberspace. A new bill that is making its way through Congress would make it illegal for companies to use medical records to create marketing lists and would grant patients access to their medical records in states that do not already do so. Mental health professionals and patient advocates across the country are debating as to whether this bill will actually advance the cause of patient privacy or precipitate a confidentiality disaster, however.

Online spying. Rich Schwerin. *PC Computing* 9:358 N '96

Almost anybody can monitor someone's on-line activity, partly due to a personal-information tracking technology known as HTML cookies. HTML cookies are small files stored on a computer that enable sites to tag a user with a unique identification. Cookies identify users by their E-mail or Internet protocol address and determine how many times a user has visited a site, which pages on the site the user visited, and other vital marketing information. Ways in which users can protect their on-line privacy are discussed.

Invasions of privacy. Jeffrey Rothfeder. *PC World* 13:152-5 + N '95

As greater amounts of confidential records are placed on distant computer networks, no information is safe from prying eyes. Medical files, financial and personnel records, Social Security numbers, telephone call records, and information about personal lifestyle preferences are available cheaply and quickly. Such records are accessible to everyone from home computer owners to real estate agents, insurance brokers, employers, private investigators, car salespeople, and marketers. In fact, information has become a hot commodity, with many state and local governments now selling, via computer, any information they have. In addition, there is an underground of information resellers that can obtain even the most sensitive data. Sidebars present information on corporate espionage, finding information about an individual, protecting personal privacy, and legislation relating to personal privacy.

Snoops. Christopher O'Malley. *Popular Science* 250:56-61 Ja '97

The marketplace for on-line information, and the capacity or desire to deliver it, are gelling at approximately the same time. Four factors have contributed to this phenomenon: PCs are everywhere today, the Internet is connecting millions of them, business and government records are stored on computers as a matter of course, and government agencies are desperately looking for new sources of revenue. Among those who want personal information about people are private investigators performing background checks or searching for deadbeat parents, lawyers tracking down court records and personal assets, prospective employers and landlords, and marketers. Advice on how to minimize one's exposure and protect on-line privacy is provided.

The good spies? Gina Smith. *Popular Science* 247:28 D '95

A number of software publishers, including Microsoft, are encouraging people to register their computer ownership by an automatic register-by-modem routine. This technology enables a hard disk to be scanned for software and hardware information, which is then sent back to the company's headquarters. With this type of information, a company can track buying habits, spy on the competition, send targeted junk mail, and determine if illegally copied software is held. It is already possible to do this kind of scanning without alerting the user, so it is not difficult to imagine the same sort of stealth technology being used on unknowing bulletin board and Internet users.

Know the code. Rick Henderson. *Reason* 28:16 Je '96

Since taking office in 1993, the Clinton administration has been in dispute with high-tech companies and privacy advocates over the use of electronic data encryption. The White House has used cold war era regulations that consider encryption to be a weapon in order to restrict the length of the encryption "keys" that can be exported without the procurement of a license from the Commerce Department. The administration plans to permit companies to sell stronger encryption programs only if the keys are placed with law enforcement or national security officials. The software industry estimates that removing these restrictions could enable U.S. companies to sell as much as $60 billion a year in encryption hardware and software by 2000. Three pending bills before Congress seek to bypass current regulations. Each would guarantee the right of Americans to use or sell whatever encryption they want domestically and would abolish export controls on any free or mass-market commercial encryption programs.

The watchers. Rick Henderson. *Reason* 27:18 N '95

In their zeal to track down parents who do not support their families, congressional welfare reformers threaten the liberty and privacy of every American. Provisions in the welfare-reform bill passed by the House this summer and a bill pending in the Senate would eventually give government employees access to personal and financial information on almost every adult. Employers would be required to register their employees' names, addresses, and social security numbers with two registries of new employees; states would be required to provide social security numbers for everyone who applies for a driving license, occupational license, marriage license, and divorce decree; and banks would be allowed to disclose individuals' financial records to state child-support agencies on request.

Privacy and data collection on the Net. Anne Eisenberg. *Scientific American* 274:120 Mr '96

Economists believe that there will come an "exponential growth in intrusiveness" as computers become faster, cheaper, and smarter. The Web is already emerging as a good source for companies that want to appeal to highly specialized interests. By analyzing clickstreams, it is possible to tell where customers are going and therefore where to advertise. Furthermore, data mining, the practice of creating programs that autonomously search data for group patterns, will inevitably come to the Internet. Despite all this electronic intrusion, there remain a few hardy individualists, privacy advocates, and Net groups who believe in untraceable communications and the technology needed to achieve it, but they will encounter a vigorous challenge with the arrival of computer telephony, or the merging of computers and telephones.

Big Brother vs. cypherpunks. Joshua Quittner. *Time* 148:78 O 14 '96

For over three years, the White House and the U.S. computer industry have argued over who will control the secret codes that protect America's most sensitive communications. The government claimed to be working to protect Americans from nuclear-weapons-wielding terrorists, and the computer industry said that it was championing the individual's right to privacy. The latest encryption initiative, which was announced recently by Vice President Al Gore, attempts to address the fears of those who object to the idea of the government holding encryption keys that the police could use to eavesdrop: The keys would be cut into a number of pieces, which would be stored with "trusted agents" of the user's choosing. Most of the large software makers—and every civil liberties group—continue to oppose the initiative, however.

Eye spy...the baby-sitter! *Time* 148:65 Jl 22 '96

Following a few widely publicized cases of horrific treatment captured on camera, the nanny-surveillance industry is booming. According to Richard Heilweil of Babywatch Corp., a Spring Valley, New York, company that sells hidden camera setups to entrepreneurs in 20 cities for rental, such surveillance rarely uncovers serious abuse or neglect. Nevertheless, about 70 percent of parents who hire Babywatch end up firing the caregiver for some minor transgression, such as talking on the phone or watching TV.

Guess who's listening. Michael Krantz. *Time* 149:30 Ja 27 '97

The boom in wireless communications has produced a corresponding boom in wireless eavesdropping. Bob Grove, publisher of the scanner journal Monitoring Times, estimates that between 10 million and 20 million people use scanning equipment to listen in on a range of wireless devices. It is extremely questionable whether all of these people's activities are ethical or even legal, however. The taping of House Speaker Newt Gingrich's cellular phone conversation with Republican allies by Democratic Party activists is discussed.

My boss, Big Brother. Jill Smolowe. *Time* 147:56 Ja 22 '96

A new law in Illinois allows employers to listen to workers' phone calls. The new state law was initially conceived by retailers and telemarketers solely to let supervisors monitor service calls for efficiency and courtesy. The measure, however, was reworked, on its way to Republican governor Jim Edgar for a December 13 signing, to embrace any listening in that serves "educational, training or research purposes" without defining unsuitable monitoring. The law is more tolerant than those in many other states and than the federal wiretap law, which orders listeners to hang up if they come across a personal call.

Intelligent highway systems vs. privacy. *USA Today* 124:14 D '95

At some point in the future, sophisticated computer-based systems will be able to tag and track cars as they travel America's highways. Proponents say that Intelligent Transportation Systems (ITS) will, among other things, improve traffic safety, reduce congestion, and save energy. According to Ohio State University professor of law Sheldon Halpern, however, ITS raises many privacy questions regarding the collection and storage of information about drivers. Such information could be used by government or private companies to build individual profiles and develop mailing lists of drivers who fit certain profiles and might be likely to purchase certain products. Although Halpern notes that current privacy law has not been designed to deal with informational privacy issues, he contends that the problems involved with ITS can be solved without complex legal changes: The technology can be designed so it does not store details about individual cars and drivers.

Marriage is not a private affair. Mary Ann Perga. *U.S. Catholic* 61:18-22 Ag '96

The most basic explanation for people's willingness to ignore domestic violence in marriages lies in the lack of understanding of the nature of marriage. Marriage has never been the private union of two lives. In fact, marriage is defined as a public commitment. People must fulfill certain criteria and obey certain rules to be married legally or to dissolve the marriage union. Civil marriage is a contract between three partners: husband, wife, and state. Christian sacramental marriage is just as communal. When a man and a woman partake of the sacrament of marriage, each one makes a promise to the other and to the church community as well. When people recognize that, as members of the state or the church, they are an essential part of any marriage, they can start to overcome their other reasons for noninvolvement. Readers' comments on the issue of marital problems are also presented.

Forget Lincoln, what about me? John Leo. *U.S. News & World Report* 120:23 Ap 29 '96

In his book Democracy's Discontent, Harvard professor Michael Sandel argues that moral norms and principles have been systematically removed from U.S. governance in just two generations. He contends that in contrast to the days of Madison or Lincoln, when laws routinely embodied the principles and views of the common good arising from the citizenry, present-day America is a "procedural republic" rooted in the idea that government should be neutral regarding the moral and religious views of its citizens. This republic frames everything in terms of individual rights, autonomy, privacy, and choice. According to Sandel, such a republic cannot support the moral energies of a vital.

It's a jungle out there. Margaret Mannix. *U.S. News & World Report* 120:73-5 Ap 29 '96

Part of cover story on the Internet. Some people act very inappropriately on the Internet and make sharp, offensive, and suggestive comments. They are wrong to assume, however, that it does not matter what they say in cyberspace. As an increasing number of people go on-line on the Internet, some users are finding that their words are being studied with a new intensity. The writer discusses etiquette, privacy, and copyright and trademark on the Internet.
democratic life.

On the griddle again. Brian Duffy. *U.S. News & World Report* 120:24-6 Ja 22 '96

Questions of candor and integrity are plaguing the Clintons. While President Clinton has had to respond to a sexual harassment lawsuit, Hillary Clinton is facing new intensified scrutiny. This has been prompted by the discovery of two sets of documents that indicate that she was more deeply involved in the 1993 firing of the White House Travel Office staff and in a peripheral legal matter than was previously disclosed. Hillary faces potential problems relating to her work in connection with the Castle Grande real estate deal, recently rediscovered billing records, and the Clintons' initial Whitewater

Development investment itself. No one, however, has documented any wrongdoing by the Clintons, and Hillary's hard-nosed tactics are attributed by her friends to her desire to protect her privacy and her reputation, not to a need to hide anything.

Our most valued right. David Gergen. *U.S. News & World Report* 120:72 Je 24 '96

The alarming revelation that a Democratic White House searched FBI files of at least 408 citizens who worked in former Republican White Houses calls not only for a full investigation but also for action to build strong walls protecting privacy in the information age. Whether the motives were innocuous or malicious, it is already obvious that the walls supposedly protecting Americans' privacy have gaping holes.

The return of the Kennedys. John Marks. *U.S. News & World Report* 121:36-8 + S 2 '96

In half a century of political and social striving, the Kennedys have become symbolic of the ebb and flow of the Democratic Party's idealism. The Kennedys are in the unequaled position of having been figures of renown since infancy, living their lives as a succession of public narratives: first as the children of enchantment, then as victims of trauma, then as examples of careless and frequently destructive behavior, and finally as embodiments of service to other people. Many of them have assumed more public roles for themselves at the same time as staunchly defending their privacy. In office, they have made their own reputations and embraced their own issues and techniques. The Kennedys are liberals whose experiences are molded much more by the inbred urge to government activism than they are moderated by the struggles of developing a business and meeting a payroll. Nonetheless, their politics must be viewed in a wider context, as the most striking aspect of their public lives is the way in which most of them have built institutions outside government.

Genetics. Harold Varmus. *Vital Speeches of the Day* 62:334-7 Mr 15 '96

In an address to the Landon Lecture Series, Kansas State University, Manhattan, Kansas, on February 5, 1996, the director of the National Institute of Health discusses new developments in the area of genetics and the ethical questions raised by these developments. The genetic revolution will produce remarkable changes in the practice of medicine, but people need to become used to the idea that their prospects for health care can be assessed early in life by genetic screening, which will lead to difficult decisions for individuals and present serious dilemmas for society. To make any further progress, an immediate political issue needs to be resolved: All states and the federal government must pass strong laws that guarantee the privacy of genetic information and protection from reprisals by insurance companies.

Values, ethics and data about people. David Van Diest Skilling. *Vital Speeches of the Day* 62:659-62 Ag 15 '96

In an address delivered to the Conference Board on Business Ethics, New York City, the executive vice president and general manager of TRW Information Systems and Services outlines his company's ethics-based approach to dealing with information about people. The company has developed, published, and shared widely five Fair Information Values. The first is partnership: The consumer represented by the data is recognized as being as much a part of the information service business as the company and the paying customer. The second is fairness: This includes openness about the means of obtaining information and the use to which it will be put. The third is balance: It is recognized that the benefit of information to the consumer must be greater than the potential harm that might arise from providing it. The fourth is education: Customers have the right to know how information about them is being collected and used. The fifth is dialogue: The company listens and responds to critics, consumers, and others.

Is the electronic eye watching you? Jose Manuel Tesoro. *World Press Review* 43:22-3 O '96

An article excerpted from the June 21 issue of *Asiaweek* of Hong Kong. Contrary to the predictions of George Orwell's *1984*, it is big business, rather than Big Brother, that is interested in monitoring people's activities. Computers can collect data to discover patterns that reveal people's habits, preferences, and even indicators about their personalities. Some information, such as one's name, address, and telephone number, is in the public domain. Other information, such as credit-card transactions or employment history, is held by private companies. There is also on record a category of so-called sensitive information, such as ethnic origin, financial holdings, nationality, religion, sexual orientation, medical history, and political and social affiliations. Unsurprisingly, a flourishing trade in personal data has emerged. The opportunities the World Wide Web offers to companies wishing to obtain personal data are discussed.

Piracy on the electronic seas. Andrew Coyne. *World Press Review* 42:9-10 Ap '95

Part of a cover story on the information superhighway. An article excerpted from the Toronto "Globe and Mail." Advances in information technology may soon make the concepts of copyright and intellectual property obsolete. Copyright protection on the information highway would probably require an intrusive degree of surveillance and intervention. Encryption and tracking technology is usually cumbersome, expensive, invasive of privacy, and vulnerable to circumvention by the clever and unscrupulous. The ultimate solution may require a redefinition of the terms of exchange, in which the original product serves as a springboard for an ongoing relationship between buyer and seller.

Video eyes are everywhere. John Naughton. World Press Review 42:13 Ap '95

Part of a cover story on the information superhighway. An article excerpted from "The Observer" of London. More than 300 local authorities in Great Britain are said to be considering or planning the introduction of video surveillance cameras in public places. Such cameras are already present in many shops, train stations, post offices, sports stadiums, and other locales. These measures have been taken with no authorizing legislation and very little public debate. Advocates of video surveillance say that it helps reduce crime and that innocent people have no reason to fear it. It will curtail everyone's privacy in the long run, however, and it is likely to increase police harassment of minorities.

Index

	DATE DUE		